MICHIKO KAKUTANI is
literary critic and the form
New York Times.

'Kakutani has written the first great book of the Trump administration. *The Death of Truth* is a fiery polemic against the president and should go down as essential reading. In nine exquisitely crafted broadsides, the Pulitzer winner calls upon her vast knowledge of literature, philosophy and politics to serve up a damning state of the union'   *Rolling Stone*

'*The Death of Truth* is destined to become the defining treatise of our age. Not only does it brilliantly and incisively diagnose the roots of our decaying social and political order; it also shows why we must rescue the truth before it is buried under a regime of lies. Everyone should read this book'   DAVID GRANN

'This book is essential reading today'

WALTER ISAACSON

'Kakutani's slender, fiery new book could have been written only by someone who reads more, and retains more, than most mere mortals'   *TIME*

'Without the truth we will be neither prosperous nor virtuous nor free. This book begins the self-defence of American culture' TIMOTHY SNYDER

'This is the book I would have written – but only if I had had a brilliant grasp of literature, politics and history, and the ability to weave them together in a uniquely original way. *The Death of Truth* goes indelibly to the dark, dark heart of what is ailing our democracy as no recent book has done' GRAYDON CARTER

'Kakutani's *The Death of Truth* is politically urgent and intellectually dazzling. She deftly goes behind the daily headlines to reveal the larger forces threatening democracy at home in America, and elsewhere around the globe. The result is a brilliant and fascinating call-to-arms that anyone who cares about democracy ought to read immediately' JANE MAYER

'An elegant polemic against Trump, tyranny and lies'
The Times

'An intellectually dazzling read' *Entertainment Weekly*

'Riveting, righteous and relevant' *Irish Times*

MICHIKO
KAKUTANI

THE DEATH OF TRUTH

WILLIAM
COLLINS

William Collins
An imprint of HarperCollins*Publishers*
1 London Bridge Street
London SE1 9GF

WilliamCollinsBooks.com

First published in Great Britain in 2018 by William Collins
First published in the United States by Tim Duggan Books,
an imprint of the Crown Publishing Group, a division of
Penguin Random House LLC, New York in 2018
This William Collins paperback edition published in 2019

1

A catalogue record for this book is
available from the British Library

ISBN 978-0-00-831280-0

Book design by Lauren Dong

Frontispiece: Truth has died, plate 79 of 'The Disasters of War', 1810–14,
pub. 1863 (etching), Goya y Lucientes, Francisco Jose de (1746–1828)/
Private Collection/Index/Bridgeman Images

Printed and bound in Great Britain by
CPI Group (UK) Ltd, Croydon

MIX
Paper from
responsible sources
FSC™ C007454

This book is produced from independently certified FSC™ paper
to ensure responsible forest management.

For more information visit: www.harpercollins.co.uk/green

For journalists everywhere working to report the news

CONTENTS

INTRODUCTION 11

1. THE DECLINE AND FALL OF REASON 21

2. THE NEW CULTURE WARS 43

3. "MOI" AND THE RISE OF
   SUBJECTIVITY 61

4. THE VANISHING OF REALITY 77

5. THE CO-OPTING OF LANGUAGE 89

6. FILTERS, SILOS, AND TRIBES 105

7. ATTENTION DEFICIT 119

8. "THE FIREHOSE OF FALSEHOOD":
   PROPAGANDA AND FAKE NEWS 135

9. THE SCHADENFREUDE OF
   THE TROLLS 151

EPILOGUE 165

NOTES 175

THE DEATH OF TRUTH

INTRODUCTION

TWO OF THE MOST MONSTROUS REGIMES in human history came to power in the twentieth century, and both were predicated upon the violation and despoiling of truth, upon the knowledge that cynicism and weariness and fear can make people susceptible to the lies and false promises of leaders bent on unconditional power. As Hannah Arendt wrote in her 1951 book, *The Origins of Totalitarianism*, "The ideal subject of totalitarian rule is not the convinced Nazi or the convinced Communist, but people for whom the distinction between fact and fiction (i.e., the reality of experience) and the distinction between true and false (i.e., the standards of thought) no longer exist."

What's alarming to the contemporary reader is that Arendt's words increasingly sound less like a dispatch from another century than a chilling mirror of the political and cultural landscape we inhabit today—a world in which fake news and lies are pumped out in industrial volume by Russian troll factories, emitted in an endless stream from the mouth and Twitter feed of the president of the United States, and sent flying across the world through social media accounts at lightning speed. Nationalism, tribalism, dislocation, fears of social change, and the hatred of outsiders are on the rise again as people, locked in their partisan silos and filter bubbles, are losing a sense of shared reality and the ability to communicate across social and sectarian lines.

This is not to draw a direct analogy between today's circumstances and the overwhelming horrors of the World War II era but to look at some of the conditions and attitudes—what Margaret Atwood has called the "danger flags" in Orwell's *1984* and *Animal Farm*—that make a people susceptible to demagoguery and political manipulation, and nations easy prey for would-be autocrats. To examine how a disregard for facts, the displacement of reason by emotion, and the corrosion of language are diminishing the very value of truth, and what that means for America and the world.

"The historian knows how vulnerable is the whole texture of facts in which we spend our daily life," Arendt wrote in a 1971 essay, "Lying in Politics"; "it is always in danger of being perforated by single lies or torn to shreds by the organized lying of groups, nations, or classes, or denied and distorted, often carefully covered up by reams of falsehoods or simply allowed to fall into oblivion. Facts need testimony to be remembered and trustworthy witnesses to be established in order to find a secure dwelling place in the domain of human affairs."

The term "truth decay" (used by the Rand Corporation to describe the "diminishing role of facts and analysis" in American public life) has joined the post-truth lexicon that includes such now familiar phrases as "fake news" and "alternative facts." And it's not just fake news either: it's also fake science (manufactured by climate change deniers and anti-vaxxers), fake history (promoted by Holocaust revisionists and white supremacists), fake Americans on Facebook (created by Russian trolls), and fake followers and "likes" on social media (generated by bots).

Trump, the forty-fifth president of the United States, lies so prolifically and with such velocity that *The Washington Post* calculated that he'd made 2,140 false or misleading claims during his first year in office—an average of nearly 5.9 a day. His lies—about everything from the investigations into Russian interference in the election, to his popularity and achievements, to how much TV he watches—are only the brightest blinking red light of many warnings of his assault on democratic institutions and norms. He routinely assails the press, the justice system, the intelligence agencies, the electoral system, and the civil servants who make our government tick.

Nor is the assault on truth confined to the United States. Around the world, waves of populism and fundamentalism are elevating appeals to fear and anger over reasoned debate, eroding democratic institutions, and replacing expertise with the wisdom of the crowd. False claims about the U.K.'s financial relationship with the EU (emblazoned on a Vote Leave campaign bus) helped swing the vote in favor of Brexit, and Russia ramped up its sowing of *dezinformatsiya* in the run-up to elections in France, Germany, the Netherlands, and other countries in concerted propaganda efforts to discredit and destabilize democracies.

Pope Francis reminded us, "There is no such thing as harmless disinformation; trusting in falsehood can have dire consequences." Former president Barack Obama observed that "one of the biggest challenges we have to our democracy is the degree to which we do not share a common baseline of facts"; people today are "operating in completely different information universes." And the Republican senator Jeff Flake gave a speech in which he warned that "2017 was a year which saw the truth—objective, empirical, evidence-based truth—more battered and abused than any other in the history of our country, at the hands of the most powerful figure in our government."

How did this happen? What are the roots of falsehood in the Trump era? How did truth and reason become such endangered species, and what does their impending demise portend for our public discourse and the future of our politics and governance? That is the subject of this book.

IT'S EASY ENOUGH to see Trump—a candidate who launched his political career on the original sin of birtherism—as a black swan who ascended to office because of a perfect storm of factors: a frustrated electorate still hurting from the backwash of the 2008 financial crash; Russian interference in the election and a deluge of pro-Trump fake news stories on social media; a highly polarizing opponent who came to symbolize the Washington elite that populists decried; and an estimated five billion dollars in free campaign coverage from media outlets obsessed with the views and clicks that the former reality-TV star generated.

If a novelist had concocted a villain like Trump—

a larger-than-life, over-the-top avatar of narcissism, mendacity, ignorance, prejudice, boorishness, demagoguery, and tyrannical impulses (not to mention someone who consumes as many as a dozen Diet Cokes a day)—she or he would likely be accused of extreme contrivance and implausibility. In fact, the president of the United States often seems less like a persuasive character than some manic cartoon artist's mashup of Ubu Roi, Triumph the Insult Comic Dog, and a character discarded by Molière.

But the more clownish aspects of Trump the personality should not blind us to the monumentally serious consequences of his assault on truth and the rule of law, and the vulnerabilities he has exposed in our institutions and digital communications. It is unlikely that a candidate who had already been exposed during the campaign for his history of lying and deceptive business practices would have gained such popular support were portions of the public not somehow blasé about truth telling and were there not more systemic problems with how people get their information and how they've come to think in increasingly partisan terms.

With Trump, the personal is political, and in many respects he is less a comic-book anomaly than an extreme, bizarro-world apotheosis of many of the broader, intertwined attitudes undermining truth today, from the merging of news and politics with entertainment, to the toxic polarization that's overtaken American politics, to the growing populist contempt for expertise.

These attitudes, in turn, are emblematic of dynamics that have been churning beneath the surface of daily life for years, creating the perfect ecosystem in which Veritas, the goddess of truth (as she was depicted by Goya in a famous print titled "Truth Has Died"), could fall mortally ill.

For decades now, objectivity—or even the idea that people can aspire toward ascertaining the best available truth—has been falling out of favor. Daniel Patrick Moynihan's well-known observation— "Everyone is entitled to his own opinion, but not to his own facts"—is more timely than ever: polarization has grown so extreme that voters in Red State America and Blue State America have a hard time even agreeing on the same facts. This has been going on since a solar system of right-wing news sites orbiting around Fox News and Breitbart News consolidated its gravitational hold over the Republican base, and it's been exponentially accelerated by social media, which connects users with like-minded members and supplies them with customized news feeds that reinforce their preconceptions, allowing them to live in ever narrower, windowless silos.

For that matter, relativism has been ascendant since the culture wars began in the 1960s. Back then, it was embraced by the New Left, eager to expose the biases of Western, bourgeois, male-dominated thinking; and by academics promoting the gospel of postmodernism, which argued that there are no universal truths, only smaller personal truths—perceptions shaped by the cultural and social forces of one's day. Since then, relativistic arguments have been hijacked by the populist Right, including creationists and climate change deniers who insist that their views be taught alongside "science-based" theories.

Relativism, of course, synced perfectly with the narcissism and subjectivity that had been on the rise, from Tom Wolfe's "Me Decade," on through the selfie age of self-esteem. No surprise then that the Rashomon effect—the point of view that everything depends on your point of view—has permeated our culture, from popular novels like *Fates and Furies*, to the television series *The Affair*, which hinge upon the idea of competing realities or unreliable narrators.

I've been reading and writing about many of these

issues for nearly four decades, going back to the rise of deconstruction and battles over the literary canon on college campuses; debates over the fictionalized retelling of history in movies like Oliver Stone's *JFK* and Kathryn Bigelow's *Zero Dark Thirty;* efforts made by both the Clinton and Bush administrations to avoid transparency and define reality on their own terms; Donald Trump's war on language and efforts to normalize the abnormal; and the consequences that technology has had on how we process and share information. In these pages, I hope to draw upon my readings of books and current events to connect some of the dots about the assault on truth and situate them in context with broader social and political dynamics that have been percolating through our culture for years. I also hope to highlight some of the prescient books and writings from the past that shed light on our current predicament.

Truth is a cornerstone of our democracy. As the former acting attorney general Sally Yates has observed, truth is one of the things that separates us from an autocracy: "We can debate policies and issues, and we should. But those debates must be based on common facts rather than raw appeals to emotion and fear through polarizing rhetoric and fabrications.

"Not only is there such a thing as objective truth,

failing to tell the truth matters. We can't control whether our public servants lie to us. But we can control whether we hold them accountable for those lies or whether, in either a state of exhaustion or to protect our own political objectives, we look the other way and normalize an indifference to truth."

1

THE DECLINE AND
FALL OF REASON

This is an apple.
Some people might try to tell you that it's a banana.
They might scream "Banana, banana, banana" over
*   and over and over again.*
They might put BANANA in all caps.
You might even start to believe that this is a banana.
But it's not.
This is an apple.

—CNN COMMERCIAL, SHOWING
A PHOTOGRAPH OF AN APPLE

N HIS 1838 LYCEUM ADDRESS, A YOUNG ABRA-
ham Lincoln spoke to his concern that as memo-
ries of the Revolution receded into the past, the
nation's liberty was threatened by a disregard for the
government's institutions, which protect the civil
and religious liberties bequeathed by the founders.
To preserve the rule of law and prevent the rise of

a would-be tyrant who might "spring up amongst us," sober reason—"cold, calculating, unimpassioned reason"—would be required. To remain "free to the last," he exhorted his audience, reason must be embraced by the American people, along with "sound morality and, in particular, a reverence for the constitution and laws."

As Lincoln well knew, the founders of America established the young republic on the Enlightenment principles of reason, liberty, progress, and religious tolerance. And the constitutional architecture they crafted was based on a rational system of checks and balances to guard against the possibility, in the words of Alexander Hamilton, of "a man unprincipled in private life" and "bold in his temper" one day arising who might "mount the hobby horse of popularity" and "flatter and fall in with all the non sense of the zealots of the day" in order to embarrass the government and "throw things into confusion that he may 'ride the storm and direct the whirlwind.'"

The system was far from perfect, but it has endured for more than two centuries thanks to its resilience and capacity to accommodate essential change. Leaders like Lincoln, Martin Luther King Jr., and Barack Obama viewed America as a work in progress—a country in the process of perfecting itself. And they tried to speed that work, mindful, in the words of Dr. King, that "progress is neither automatic nor inevitable" but requiring of continuous dedication and struggle. What had been achieved since the Civil War and the civil rights movement was a reminder of all the work yet to be done, but also a testament to President Obama's faith that Americans "can constantly remake ourselves to fit our larger dreams," and the Enlightenment faith in what George Washington called the great "experiment entrusted to the hands of the American people."

Alongside this optimistic vision of America as a nation that could become a shining "city upon a hill," there's also been a dark, irrational counter-theme in U.S. history, which has now reasserted itself with a vengeance—to the point where reason not only is being undermined but seems to have been tossed out the window, along with facts, informed debate, and deliberative policy making. Science is under attack, and so is expertise of every sort—be it expertise in foreign policy, national security, economics, or education.

Philip Roth called this counternarrative "the indigenous American berserk," and the historian Richard Hofstadter famously described it as "the paranoid style"—an outlook animated by "heated exaggeration, suspiciousness, and conspiratorial fantasy" and focused on perceived threats to "a nation, a culture, a way of life." Hofstadter's 1964 essay was spurred by Barry Goldwater's campaign and the right-wing movement around it, just as his 1963 book, *Anti-intellectualism in American Life,* was conceived in response to Senator Joseph McCarthy's notorious witch hunts and the larger political and social backdrop of the 1950s.

Goldwater lost his presidential bid, and McCarthyism burned itself out after a lawyer for the U.S. Army, Joseph Welch, had the courage to stand up to McCarthy. "Have you no sense of decency, sir, at long last?" Welch asked. "Have you left no sense of decency?"

The venomous McCarthy, who hurled accusations of disloyalty throughout Washington ("the State Department harbors a nest of Communists and Communist sympathizers," he warned President Truman in 1950), was rebuked by the Senate in 1954, and with the Soviets' launch of Sputnik in 1957 the menacing antirationalism of the day began to recede, giving way to the space race and a concerted effort to improve the nation's science programs.

Hofstadter observed that the paranoid style tends to occur in "episodic waves." The anti-Catholic, anti-immigrant Know-Nothing Party reached its height in 1855, with forty-three members of Congress openly avowing their allegiance. Its power quickly began to dissipate the following year, after the party split along sectional lines, though the intolerance it embodied would remain, like a virus, in the political system, waiting to reemerge.

In the case of the modern right wing, Hofstadter argued that it tended to be mobilized by a sense of grievance and dispossession. "America has been largely taken away from them," he wrote, and they may feel that "they have no access to political bargaining or the making of decisions."

In the case of millennial-era America (and much of western Europe, too), these were grievances exacerbated by changing demographics and changing social mores that had made some members of the white working class feel increasingly marginalized; by growing income inequalities accelerated by the financial crisis of 2008; and by forces like globalization and technology that were stealing manufacturing jobs and injecting daily life with a new uncertainty and angst.

Trump and nationalist, anti-immigrant leaders on the right in Europe like Marine Le Pen in France, Geert Wilders in the Netherlands, and Matteo Salvini in Italy would inflame these feelings of fear and anger and disenfranchisement, offering scapegoats instead of solutions; while liberals and conservatives, worried about the rise of nativism and the politics of prejudice, warned that democratic institutions were coming under growing threat. Yeats's poem "The Second Coming," written in 1919, amid the wreckage of World War I, experienced a huge revival in 2016—quoted, in news articles, more in the first half of that year than it had been in three decades as commentators of all political persuasions invoked its famous lines: "Things fall apart; the centre cannot hold; / Mere anarchy is loosed upon the world."

The assault on truth and reason that reached fever pitch in America during the first year of the Trump presidency had been incubating for years on the fringe right. Clinton haters who were manufacturing nutty accusations about the death of Vince Foster in the 1990s and Tea Party paranoids who claimed that environmentalists wanted to control the temperature of your home and the color of cars you can buy hooked up, during the 2016 campaign, with Breitbart bloggers and alt-right trolls. And with Trump's winning of the Republican nomination and the presidency, the extremist views of his most radical supporters—their racial and religious intolerance, their detestation of government, and their embrace of conspiracy thinking and misinformation—went mainstream.

According to a 2017 survey by *The Washington*

Post, 47 percent of Republicans erroneously believe that Trump won the popular vote, 68 percent believe that millions of illegal immigrants voted in 2016, and more than half of Republicans say they would be okay with postponing the 2020 presidential election until such problems with illegal voting can be fixed. Another study conducted by political scientists at the University of Chicago showed that 25 percent of Americans believe that the 2008 crash was secretly orchestrated by a small cabal of bankers, 19 percent believe that the U.S. government had a hand in the 9/11 terrorist attacks, and 11 percent even believe a theory made up by the researchers—that compact fluorescent lightbulbs were part of a government plot to make people more passive and easy to control.

Trump, who launched his political career by shamelessly promoting birtherism and who has spoken approvingly of the conspiracy theorist and shock jock Alex Jones, presided over an administration that became, in its first year, the very embodiment of anti-Enlightenment principles, repudiating the values of rationalism, tolerance, and empiricism in both its policies and its modus operandi—a reflection of the commander in chief's erratic, impulsive decision-making style based not on knowledge but on instinct, whim, and preconceived (and often delusional) notions of how the world operates.

Trump made no effort to rectify his ignorance of domestic and foreign policy when he moved into the White House. His former chief strategist Stephen Bannon has said that Trump only "reads to reinforce"; and the president has remained determined to deny, diminish, or downplay intelligence concerning Russian interference in the 2016 election. Because such mentions tend to draw his ire and can disrupt his intelligence briefings, officials told *The Washington Post* that they sometimes included this material only in written versions of the president's daily brief, which he reportedly rarely if ever reads.

Instead, the president seems to prefer getting his information from Fox News—in particular, the sycophantic morning show *Fox & Friends*—and from sources like Breitbart News and the *National Enquirer*. He reportedly spends as much as eight hours a day watching television—a habit that could not help but remind many readers of Chauncey Gardiner, the TV-addicted gardener who becomes a celebrity and rising political star in Jerzy Kosinski's 1970 novel, *Being There*. Vice News also reported that Trump received a folder, twice a day, filled with flattering clips including "admiring tweets, transcripts of fawning TV interviews, praise-filled news stories, and sometimes just pictures of Trump on TV looking powerful."

Such absurd details are unnerving rather than merely comical because this is not simply a *Twilight Zone* case of one fantasist living in a big white house in Washington, D.C. Trump's proclivity for chaos has not been contained by those around him but has instead infected his entire administration. He asserts that "I'm the only one that matters" when it comes to policy making, and given his disdain for institutional knowledge he frequently ignores the advice of cabinet members and agencies, when he isn't cutting them out of the loop entirely.

Ironically, the dysfunction that these habits fuel tends to ratify his supporters' mistrust of Washington (one of the main reasons they voted for Trump in the first place), creating a kind of self-fulfilling prophecy, which, in turn, breeds further cynicism and a reluctance to participate in the political process. A growing number of voters feel there is a gross disconnect between their views and government policies. Commonsense policies like mandatory background checks for gun purchases, supported by more than nine out of ten Americans, have been stymied by Congress, which is filled with members who rely on donations from the NRA. Eighty-seven percent of Americans said in a 2018 poll that they believe Dreamers should be allowed to stay in the States, and yet DACA has remained a political football. And 83 percent of Americans (including 75 percent of Republicans) say they support net neutrality, which was overturned by Trump's FCC.

THE DECLINING ROLE of rational discourse—and the diminished role of common sense and fact-based policy—hardly started with Donald J. Trump. Rather, he represents the culmination of trends diagnosed in prescient books by Al Gore, Farhad Manjoo, and Susan Jacoby, published nearly a decade before he took up residence at 1600 Pennsylvania Avenue. Among the causes of this decline, Jacoby (*The Age of American Unreason*) cited an "addiction to infotainment," the continuing strength of religious fundamentalism, "the popular equation of intellectualism with a liberalism supposedly at odds with traditional American values," and an education system that "does a poor job of teaching not only basic skills but the logic underlying those skills."

As for Gore (*The Assault on Reason*), he underscored the ailing condition of America as a participatory democracy (low voter turnout, an ill-informed electorate, campaigns dominated by money, and media manipulation) and "the persistent and sustained reliance on falsehoods as the basis of policy, even in the face of massive and well-understood evidence to the contrary."

At the forefront of Gore's thinking was the Bush administration's disastrous decision to invade Iraq and its cynical selling of that war to the public, distorting "America's political reality by creating a new fear of Iraq that was hugely disproportionate to the actual danger" posed by a country that did not attack the United States on 9/11 and lacked the terrifying weapons of mass destruction that administration hawks scared Americans into thinking it possessed.

Indeed, the Iraq war remains a lesson in the calamities that can result when momentous decisions that affect the entire world are not made through a rational policy-making process and the judicious weighing of information and expert analysis, but are instead fueled by ideological certainty and the cherry picking of intelligence to support preconceived idées fixes.

From the start, administration hawks led by Vice President Dick Cheney and Secretary of Defense Donald Rumsfeld pressed for "forward-leaning" intelligence that would help make the case for war. A shadowy operation called the Office of Special

Plans was even set up at the Defense Department; its mission, according to a Pentagon adviser quoted by Seymour M. Hersh in *The New Yorker*, was to find evidence of what Rumsfeld and Deputy Secretary of Defense Paul Wolfowitz already believed to be true—that Saddam Hussein had ties to al-Qaeda and that Iraq possessed a huge arsenal of biological, chemical, and possibly nuclear weapons.

Meanwhile, planning for the war on the ground ignored sober warnings from experts, like the army chief of staff, Eric K. Shinseki, who testified that postwar Iraq would require "something on the order of several hundred thousand soldiers." His recommendation was quickly shot down, as were reports from the Rand Corporation and the Army War College, both of which also warned that postwar security and reconstruction in Iraq would require a large number of troops for an extended period of time. These assessments went unheeded—with fateful consequences—because they did not mesh with the administration's willfully optimistic promises that the Iraqi people would welcome American troops as liberators and that resistance on the ground would be limited. "A cakewalk," as one Rumsfeld ally put it.

The failure to send enough troops to secure the

country and restore law and order; the sidelining of the State Department's Future of Iraq Project (because of tensions with the Pentagon); the ad hoc decisions to dissolve the Iraqi army and to ban all senior members of the Baath Party: such disastrous and avoidable screwups resulted in a bungled American occupation that one soldier, assigned to the Coalition Provisional Authority, memorably described as "pasting feathers together, hoping for a duck." In fact, the Iraq war would prove to be one of the young century's most catastrophic events, exploding the geopolitics of the region and giving birth to ISIS and a still unspooling set of disasters for the people of Iraq, the region, and the world.

ALTHOUGH TRUMP frequently criticized the decision to invade Iraq during the 2016 campaign, his White House has learned nothing from the Bush administration's handling of that unnecessary and tragic war. Instead, it has doubled down on reverse-engineered policy making and the repudiation of experts.

For instance, the State Department has been hollowed out as a result of Steve Bannon's vow to fight for the "deconstruction of the administrative state" and the White House's suspicion of "deep state" professionals. The president's son-in-law, Jared Kushner, a thirty-six-year-old real-estate developer with no government experience, was handed the Middle East portfolio, while the shrinking State Department was increasingly sidelined. Many important positions stood unfilled at the end of Trump's first year in office. This was partly because of downsizing and dereliction of duty, partly because of a reluctance to appoint diplomats who expressed reservations about the president's policies (as in the case of the crucial role of ambassador to South Korea), and partly because of the exodus of foreign service talent from an agency that, under new management, no longer valued their skills at diplomacy, policy knowledge, or experience in far-flung regions of the world. Combined with Trump's subversion of longtime alliances and trade accords and his steady undermining of democratic ideals, the carelessness with which his administration treated foreign policy led to world confidence in U.S. leadership plummeting in 2017 to a new low of 30 percent (below China and just above Russia), according to a Gallup poll.

In some respects, the Trump White House's disdain for expertise and experience reflected larger attitudes percolating through American society. In his 2007 book, *The Cult of the Amateur*, the Silicon Valley entrepreneur Andrew Keen warned that the internet not only had democratized information beyond people's wildest imaginings but also was replacing genuine knowledge with "the wisdom of the crowd," dangerously blurring the lines between fact and opinion, informed argument and blustering speculation.

A decade later, the scholar Tom Nichols wrote in *The Death of Expertise* that a willful hostility toward established knowledge had emerged on both the right and the left, with people aggressively arguing that "every opinion on any matter is as good as every other." Ignorance now was fashionable.

"If citizens do not bother to gain basic literacy in the issues that affect their lives," Nichols wrote, "they abdicate control over those issues whether they like it or not. And when voters lose control of these important decisions, they risk the hijacking of their democracy by ignorant demagogues, or the more quiet and gradual decay of their democratic institutions into authoritarian technocracy."

THE TRUMP White House's preference for loyalty and ideological lockstep over knowledge is on display throughout the administration. Unqualified judges and agency heads were appointed because of cronyism, political connections, or a determination to undercut agencies that stood in the way of Trump's massive deregulatory plans benefiting the fossil fuel industry and wealthy corporate donors. Rick Perry, who was famous for wanting to abolish the Department of Energy, was named to head it, presiding over cutbacks to renewable energy programs; and the new EPA head, Scott Pruitt, who had repeatedly sued the Environmental Protection Agency over the years, swiftly began dismantling and slow walking legislation designed to protect the environment.

The public—which opposed the GOP tax bill and worried that its health care would be taken away—was high-handedly ignored when its views failed to accord with Trump administration objectives or those of the Republican Congress. And when experts in a given field—like climate change, fiscal policy, or national security—raised inconvenient questions, they were sidelined, or worse. This, for instance, is what happened to the Congressional Budget Office (created decades ago as an independent, nonpartisan provider of cost estimates for legislation) when it reported that a proposed GOP health-care bill would leave millions more uninsured. Republicans began attacking the agency—not just its report, but its very existence. Trump's director of the Office of Management and Budget, Mick Mulvaney, asked whether the CBO's time had "come and gone," and other Republicans proposed slashing its budget and cutting its staff of 235 by 89 employees.

For that matter, the normal machinery of policy making—and the normal process of analysis and review—were routinely circumvented by the Trump administration, which violated such norms with knee-jerk predictability. Many moves were the irrational result of a kind of reverse engineering: deciding on an outcome the White House or the Republican Congress wanted, then trying to come up with rationales or selling points afterward. This was the very opposite of the scientific method, whereby data is systematically gathered and assessed to formulate and test hypotheses—a method the administration clearly had contempt for, given its orders to CDC analysts to avoid using the terms "science-based" and "evidence-based." And it was a reminder that in Orwell's dystopia in *1984* there is no word for "science," because "the empirical method of thought, on which all the scientific achievements of the past were founded," represents an objective reality that threatens the power of Big Brother to determine what truth is.

In addition to announcing that it was withdrawing from the Paris climate accord (after Syria signed on, the United States was left as the lone country repudiating the global agreement), the Trump administration vowed to terminate President Obama's Clean Power Plan and reverse a ban on offshore oil and gas drilling. Scientists were dismissed from government advisory boards, and plans were made to cut funding for an array of research programs in such fields as biomedicine, environmental science, engineering, and data analysis. The EPA alone was facing proposed cuts from the White House of $2.5 billion from its annual budget—a reduction of more than 23 percent.

IN APRIL 2017, the March for Science, organized in Washington to protest the Trump administration's antiscience policies, grew into more than four hundred marches in more than thirty-five nations, participants marching out of solidarity with colleagues in the United States and also out of concern for the status of science and reason in their own countries. Decisions made by the U.S. government about climate change and other global problems, after all, have a domino effect around the world—affecting joint enterprises and collaborative research, as well as efforts to find international solutions to crises affecting the planet.

British scientists worry about how Brexit will affect universities and research institutions in the U.K. and the ability of British students to study in Europe. Scientists in countries from Australia to Germany to Mexico worry about the spread of attitudes devaluing science, evidence, and peer review. And doctors in Latin America and Africa worry that fake news about Zika and Ebola are spreading misinformation and fear.

Mike MacFerrin, a graduate student in glaciology working in Kangerlussuaq, a town of five hundred in Greenland, told *Science* magazine that the residents there had practical reasons to worry about climate change because runoff from the ice sheet had partially washed out a local bridge. "I liken the attacks on science to turning off the headlights," he said. "We're driving fast and people don't want to see what's coming up. Scientists—we're the headlights."

ONE OF THE most harrowing accounts of just how quickly "the rule of *raison*"—faith in science, humanism, progress, and liberty—can give way to "its very opposite, terror and mass emotion," was laid out by the Austrian writer Stefan Zweig in his 1942 memoir, *The World of Yesterday*. Zweig witnessed two globe-shaking calamities in his life—World War I, followed by a brief respite, and then the cataclysmic rise of Hitler and descent into World War II. His memoir is an act of bearing witness to how Europe tore itself apart suicidally twice within decades—the story of the terrible "defeat of reason" and "the wildest triumph of brutality," and a lesson, he hoped, for future generations.

Zweig wrote about growing up in a place and time when the miracles of science—the conquest of diseases, "the transmission of the human word in a second around the globe"—made progress seem inevitable, and even dire problems like poverty "no longer seemed insurmountable." An optimism (which may remind some readers of the hopes that surged through the Western world after the fall of the Berlin Wall in 1989) informed his father's generation, Zweig recalled: "They honestly believed that the divergencies and the boundaries between nations and sects would gradually melt away into a common humanity and that peace and security, the highest of treasures, would be shared by all mankind."

When he was young, Zweig and his friends spent hours hanging out at coffeehouses, talking about art and personal concerns: "We had a passion to be the first to discover the latest, the newest, the most extravagant, the unusual." There was a sense of security in those years for the upper and middle classes: "One's house was insured against fire and theft, one's field against hail and storm, one's person against accident and sickness."

People were slow to recognize the danger Hitler represented. "The few among writers who had taken the trouble to read Hitler's book," Zweig writes, "ridiculed the bombast of his stilted prose instead of occupying themselves with his program." Newspapers reassured readers that the Nazi movement would "collapse in no time." And many assumed that if "an anti-semitic agitator" actually did become chancellor, he "would as a matter of course throw off such vulgarities."

Ominous signs were piling up. Groups of menacing young men near the German border "preached their gospel to the accompaniment of threats that whoever did not join promptly, would have to pay for it later." And "the underground cracks and crevices between the classes and races, which the age of conciliation had so laboriously patched up," were breaking open again and soon "widened into abysses and chasms."

But the Nazis were careful, Zweig remembers, not to disclose the full extent of their aims right away. "They practiced their method carefully: only a small dose to begin with, then a brief pause. Only a single pill at a time and then a moment of waiting to observe the effect of its strength"—to see whether the public and the "world conscience would still digest this dose."

And because they were reluctant to abandon their accustomed lives, their daily routines and habits, Zweig wrote, people did not want to believe how rapidly their freedoms were being stolen. People asked what Germany's new leader could possibly "put through by force in a State where law was securely anchored, where the majority in parliament was against him, and where every citizen believed his liberty and equal rights secured by the solemnly affirmed constitution"—this eruption of madness, they told themselves, "could not last in the twentieth century."

2

THE NEW CULTURE
WARS

*The death of objectivity "relieves me of the
obligation to be right." It "demands only that I be
interesting."*

—STANLEY FISH

N A PRESCIENT 2005 ARTICLE, DAVID FOSTER
Wallace wrote that the proliferation of news outlets—
in print, on TV, and online—had created "a kaleidoscope of information options." Wallace observed that
one of the ironies of this strange media landscape
that had given birth to a proliferation of ideological
news outlets (including so many on the right, like
Fox News and *The Rush Limbaugh Show*) was that it
created "precisely the kind of relativism that cultural
conservatives decry, a kind of epistemic free-for-all in
which 'the truth' is wholly a matter of perspective and
agenda."

Those words were written more than a decade before the election of 2016, and they uncannily predict the post-Trump cultural landscape, where truth increasingly seems to be in the eye of the beholder, facts are fungible and socially constructed, and we often feel as if we've been transported to an upside-down world where assumptions and alignments in place for decades have suddenly been turned inside out.

The Republican Party, once a bastion of Cold War warriors, and Trump, who ran on a law-and-order platform, shrug off the dangers of Russia's meddling in American elections, and GOP members of Congress talk about secret cabals within the FBI and the Department of Justice. Like some members of the 1960s counterculture, many of these new Republicans reject rationality and science. During the first round of the culture wars, many on the new left rejected Enlightenment ideals as vestiges of old patriarchal and imperialist thinking. Today, such ideals of reason and progress are assailed on the right as part of a liberal plot to undercut traditional values or suspicious signs of egghead, eastern-corridor elitism. For that matter, paranoia about the government has increasingly migrated from the Left—which blamed the military-industrial complex for Vietnam—to the Right, with alt-right trolls and Republican members of Congress now blaming the so-called deep state for plotting against the president.

The Trump campaign depicted itself as an insurgent, revolutionary force, battling on behalf of its marginalized constituency and disingenuously using language which strangely echoed that used by radicals in the 1960s. "We're trying to disrupt the collusion between the wealthy donors, the large corporations, and the media executives," Trump declared at one rally. And in another he called for replacing this "failed and corrupt political establishment."

More ironic still is the populist Right's appropriation of postmodernist arguments and its embrace of the philosophical repudiation of objectivity—schools of thought affiliated for decades with the Left and with the very elite academic circles that Trump and company scorn. Why should we care about these often arcane-sounding arguments from academia? It's safe to say that Trump has never plowed through the works of Derrida, Baudrillard, or Lyotard (if he's even heard of them), and postmodernists are hardly to blame for all the free-floating nihilism abroad in the land. But some dumbed-down corollaries of their thinking have seeped into popular culture and been hijacked by the president's defenders, who want to use its relativistic arguments to excuse his lies, and by right-wingers who want to question evolution or deny the reality of climate change or promote alternative facts. Even Mike Cernovich, the notorious alt-right troll and conspiracy theorist, invoked postmodernism in a 2016 interview with *The New Yorker*. "Look, I read postmodernist theory in college. If everything is a narrative, then we need alternatives to the dominant narrative," he said, adding, "I don't seem like a guy who reads Lacan, do I?"

SINCE THE 1960S, there has been a snowballing loss of faith in institutions and official narratives. Some of this skepticism has been a necessary corrective—a rational response to the calamities of Vietnam and Iraq, to Watergate and the financial crisis of 2008, and to the cultural biases that had long infected everything from the teaching of history in elementary schools to the injustices of the justice system. But the liberating democratization of information made possible by the internet not only spurred breathtaking innovation and entrepreneurship; it also led to a cascade of misinformation and relativism, as evidenced by today's fake news epidemic.

Central to the breakdown of official narratives in academia was the constellation of ideas falling under the broad umbrella of postmodernism, which arrived at American universities in the second half of the twentieth century via such French theorists as Foucault and Derrida (whose ideas, in turn, were indebted to the German philosophers Heidegger and Nietzsche). In literature, film, architecture, music, and painting, postmodernist concepts (exploding storytelling traditions and breaking down boundaries between genres, and between popular culture and high art) would prove emancipating and in some cases transformative, resulting in a wide range of innovative works from artists like Thomas Pynchon, David Bowie, the Coen brothers, Quentin Tarantino, David Lynch, Paul Thomas Anderson, and Frank Gehry. When postmodernist theories were applied to the social sciences and history, however, all sorts of philosophical implications, both intended and unintended, would result and eventually pinball through our culture.

There are many different strands of postmodernism and many different interpretations, but very broadly speaking, postmodernist arguments deny an objective reality existing independently from human perception, contending that knowledge is filtered through the prisms of class, race, gender, and other variables. In rejecting the possibility of an objective reality and substituting the notions of perspective and positioning for the idea of truth, postmodernism enshrined the principle of subjectivity. Language is seen as unreliable and unstable (part of the unbridgeable gap between what is said and what is meant), and even the notion of people acting as fully rational, autonomous individuals is discounted, as each of us is shaped, consciously or unconsciously, by a particular time and culture.

Out with the idea of consensus. Out with the view of history as a linear narrative. Out with big universal or transcendent meta-narratives. The Enlightenment, for instance, is dismissed by many postmodernists on the left as a hegemonic or Eurocentric reading of history, aimed at promoting colonialist or capitalistic notions of reason and progress. The Christian narrative of redemption is rejected, too, as is the Marxist road to a Communist utopia. To some postmodernists, the scholar Christopher Butler observes, even the arguments of scientists can be "seen as no more than quasi narratives which compete with all the others for acceptance. They have no unique or reliable fit to the world, no certain correspondence with reality. They are just another form of fiction."

THE MIGRATION OF postmodern ideas from academia to the political mainstream is a reminder of how the culture wars—as the vociferous debates over race, religion, gender, and school curricula were called during the 1980s and 1990s—have mutated in unexpected ways. The terrorist attacks of 9/11 and the financial crisis of 2008, it was thought, had marginalized those debates, and there was hope, during the second term of President Barack Obama, that the culture wars in their most virulent form might be winding down. Health-care legislation, the Paris climate accord, a stabilizing economy after the crash of 2008, same-sex marriage, efforts to address the inequities of the criminal justice system—although a lot of essential reforms remained to be done, many Americans believed that the country was at least set on a progressive path.

In his 2015 book, *A War for the Soul of America*, the historian Andrew Hartman wrote that the traditionalists who "resisted the cultural changes set into motion during the sixties" and "identified with the normative Americanism of the 1950s" seemed to have lost the culture wars of the 1980s and 1990s. By the twenty-first century, Hartman wrote, "a growing majority of Americans now accept and even embrace what at the time seemed like a new nation. In this light, the late-twentieth-century culture wars should be understood as an adjustment period. The nation struggled over cultural change in order to adjust to it. The culture wars compelled Americans, even conservatives, to acknowledge transformations to American life. And although acknowledgment often came in the form of rejection, it was also the first step to resignation, if not outright acceptance."

As it turns out, this optimistic assessment was radically premature, much the way that Francis Fukuyama's 1989 essay "The End of History?" (arguing that with the implosion of Soviet Communism liberal democracy had triumphed and would become "the final form of human government") was premature. A Freedom House report concluded that "with populist and nationalist forces making significant gains in democratic states, 2016 marked the eleventh consecutive year of decline in global freedom." And in 2017, Fukuyama said he was concerned about "a slow erosion of institutions" and democratic norms under President Trump; twenty-five years earlier, he said, he "didn't have a sense or a theory about how democracies can go backward" but now realized "they clearly can."

As for the culture wars, they quickly came roaring back. Hard-core segments of the Republican base—

the Tea Party, birthers, right-wing evangelicals, white nationalists—had mobilized against President Obama and his policies. And Trump, as both candidate and president, would pour gasoline on these social and political fractures—as a way to both gin up his base and distract attention from his policy failures and many scandals. He exploited the partisan divides in American society, appealing to the fears of white working-class voters worried about a changing world, while giving them scapegoats he selected—immigrants, African Americans, women, Muslims—as targets for their anger. It's no coincidence that Russian trolls—working to get Trump elected while trying to undermine faith in the U.S. democratic system—were, at the same time, using fake social media accounts in efforts to further amplify divisions among Americans. For instance, it turned out that Russian trolls used an impostor Facebook account called "Heart of Texas" to organize a protest called "Stop the Islamization of Texas" in May 2016 and another impostor Facebook account called "United Muslims of America" to organize a counterprotest at the same time and place.

Some of the most eloquent critics of Trump's politics of fear and division have been conservatives like Steve Schmidt, Nicolle Wallace, Joe Scarborough, Jennifer Rubin, Max Boot, David Frum, Bill Kristol,

Michael Gerson, and the Republican senators John McCain and Jeff Flake. But most of the GOP rallied behind Trump, rationalizing his lies, his disdain for expertise, his contempt for many of the very ideals America was founded upon. For such Trump enablers, party trumped everything—morality, national security, fiscal responsibility, common sense, and common decency. In the wake of stories about Trump's alleged affair with the porn star Stormy Daniels, evangelicals came to his defense: Jerry Falwell Jr. said "all these things were years ago," and Tony Perkins, president of the Family Research Council, said he and his supporters were willing to give Trump a pass for his personal behavior.

It's an ironic development, given where conservatives stood during the first wave of the culture wars in the 1980s and 1990s. Back then, it was conservatives who promoted themselves as guardians of tradition, expertise, and the rule of law, standing in opposition to what they saw as the decline of reason and a repudiation of Western values. In his 1987 book, *The Closing of the American Mind*, the political philosophy professor Allan Bloom railed against relativism and condemned 1960s campus protests in which, he said, "commitment was understood to be profounder than science, passion than reason." And the scholar

Gertrude Himmelfarb warned that the writing and teaching of history had been politicized by a new generation of postmodernists: in viewing the past through the lenses of variables like gender and race, she argued, postmodernists were implying not just that all truths are contingent but that "it is not only futile but positively baneful to aspire to them."

Some critics unfairly tried to lump the pluralistic impulses of multiculturalism together with the arguments of radical postmodernists who mocked the very possibility of teaching (or writing) history fairly. The former offered a crucial antidote to traditional narratives of American exceptionalism and Western triumphalism by opening the once narrow gates of history to the voices of women, African Americans, Native Americans, immigrants, and other heretofore marginalized points of view. Multiculturalism underscored the incompleteness of much history writing, as Joyce Appleby, Lynn Hunt, and Margaret Jacob argued in their incisive and common-sense-filled book, *Telling the Truth About History*, and offered the possibility of a more inclusive, more choral perspective. But they also warned that extreme views could lead to the dangerously reductive belief that "knowledge about the past is simply an ideological construction intended to serve particular interests, making history a series of myths establishing or reinforcing group identities."

Science, too, came under attack by radical postmodernists, who argued that scientific theories are socially constructed: they are informed by the identity of the person positing the theory and the values of the culture in which they are formed; therefore, science cannot possibly make claims to neutrality or universal truths.

"The postmodern view fit well with the ambivalence toward science that developed after the bomb and during the Cold War," Shawn Otto wrote in *The War on Science*. Among left-leaning academics in the humanities departments of universities, he went on, "science came to be seen as the province of a hawkish, pro-business, right-wing power structure—polluting, uncaring, greedy, mechanistic, sexist, racist, imperialist, homophobic, oppressive, intolerant. A heartless ideology that cared little for the spiritual or holistic wellness of our souls, our bodies, or our Mother Earth."

It was ridiculous, of course, to argue that a researcher's cultural background could affect verifiable scientific facts; as Otto succinctly put it, "Atmospheric CO_2 is the same whether the scientist measuring it is a Somali woman or an Argentine man." But such postmodernist arguments would clear the way for to-day's anti-vaxxers and global warming deniers, who refuse to accept the consensus opinion of the over-whelming majority of scientists.

As on so many other subjects, Orwell saw the perils of this sort of thinking decades ago. In a 1943 essay, he wrote, "What is peculiar to our own age is the abandonment of the idea that history *could* be truthfully written. In the past people deliberately lied, or they unconsciously coloured what they wrote, or they struggled after the truth, well knowing that they must make many mistakes; but in each case they believed that 'facts' existed and were more or less dis-coverable."

"It is just this common basis of agreement," he went on, "with its implication that human beings are all one species of animal, that totalitarianism destroys. Nazi theory indeed specifically denies that such a thing as 'the truth' exists. There is, for instance, no such thing as 'Science.' There is only 'German Science,' 'Jewish Science,' etc." When truth is so fragmented, so rela-tive, Orwell noted, a path is opened for some "Leader, or some ruling clique" to dictate what is to be be-lieved: "If the Leader says of such and such an event, 'It never happened'—well, it never happened."

People trying to win respectability for clearly

discredited theories—or, in the case of Holocaust revisionists, trying to whitewash entire chapters of history—exploited the postmodernist argument that all truths are partial. Deconstructionist history, the scholar Deborah E. Lipstadt observed in *Denying the Holocaust*, has "the potential to alter dramatically the way established truth is transmitted from generation to generation." And it can foster an intellectual climate in which "no fact, no event, and no aspect of history has any fixed meaning or content. Any truth can be retold. Any fact can be recast. There is no ultimate historical reality."

POSTMODERNISM NOT ONLY rejected all metanarratives but also emphasized the instability of language. One of postmodernism's founding fathers, Jacques Derrida—who would achieve celebrity status on American campuses in the 1970s and 1980s thanks in large part to such disciples as Paul de Man and J. Hillis Miller—used the word "deconstruction" to describe the sort of textual analysis he pioneered that would be applied not just to literature but to history, architecture, and the social sciences as well.

Deconstruction posited that all texts are unstable and irreducibly complex and that ever variable meanings are imputed by readers and observers. In focusing on the possible contradictions and ambiguities of a text (and articulating such arguments in deliberately tangled and pretentious prose), it promulgated an extreme relativism that was ultimately nihilistic in its implications: anything could mean anything; an author's intent did not matter, could not in fact be discerned; there was no such thing as an obvious or common-sense reading, because everything had an infinitude of meanings. In short, there was no such thing as truth.

As David Lehman recounted in his astute book *Signs of the Times*, the worst suspicions of critics of deconstruction were confirmed when the Paul de Man scandal exploded in 1987 and deconstructionist rationales were advanced to defend the indefensible.

De Man, a professor at Yale and one of deconstruction's brightest stars, had achieved an almost cultlike following in academic circles. Students and colleagues described him as a brilliant, charismatic, and charming scholar who had fled Nazi Europe, where, he implied, he had been a member of the Belgian Resistance. A very different portrait would emerge from Evelyn Barish's biography *The Double Life of Paul de Man*: an unrepentant con man—an opportunist, bigamist, and toxic narcissist who'd been convicted in Belgium of fraud, forgery, and falsifying records.

The most shocking news had been revealed in 1987, four years after his death: a young Belgian researcher discovered that de Man had written at least one hundred articles for a pro-Nazi Belgian publication, *Le Soir*, during World War II—a publication that espoused a virulent anti-Semitism, declaring in one editorial that "we are determined to forbid ourselves any cross-breeding with them and to liberate ourselves spiritually from their demoralizing influence in the realm of thought, literature, and the arts."

In the most notorious of his *Le Soir* articles, de Man argued that "Jewish writers have always remained in the second rank" and had therefore failed to exercise "a preponderant influence" on the evolution of contemporary European civilization. "One can thus see," he wrote, "that a solution to the Jewish problem that would lead to the creation of a Jewish colony isolated from Europe would not have, for the literary life of the West, regrettable consequences. It would lose, in all, some personalities of mediocre worth and would continue, as in the past, to develop according to its higher laws of evolution."

As news of de Man's alarming collaborationist writings swept through academia, some scholars wondered if de Man's shameful and secret past had informed his theories about deconstruction—for instance, his contention that "considerations of the actual and historical existence of writers are a waste of time."

More disturbing still were efforts by some of de Man's defenders, like Derrida, to use the principles of deconstruction to try to explain away de Man's anti-Semitic writings, suggesting that his words actually subverted what they appeared to say or that there was too much ambiguity inherent in his words to assign moral responsibility.

One de Man admirer, cited by Lehman, tried to argue that de Man's remarks about Jewish writers were a case of "irony" misfiring, contending that the essay's tone was "one of detached mockery throughout the sections dealing with the Jews, and the object of the mockery is clearly not the Jews but rather the anti-Semites." In other words, the writer was suggesting that de Man had meant the very opposite of what his *Le Soir* columns stated.

Though deconstructionists are fond of employing jargon-filled prose and perversely acrobatic syntax, some of the terms they use—like the "indeterminacy of texts," "alternative ways of knowing," and the "linguistic instability" of language—feel like pretentious versions of phrases recently used by Trump aides to explain away his lies, flip-flops, and bad-faith promises. For instance: a Trump representative telling an adviser to the Japanese prime minister, Shinzo Abe, that they didn't "have to take each word that Mr. Trump said publicly literally"; and a former campaign manager, Corey Lewandowski, asserting that the problem with the media is "You guys took everything Donald Trump said so literally. The American people didn't."

3

"MOI" AND THE RISE OF SUBJECTIVITY

Our subjectivity is so completely our own.

—SPIKE JONZE

PARALLEL WITH ACADEMIA'S EMBRACE OF postmodernism was the blossoming in the 1970s of what Christopher Lasch called "the culture of narcissism" and what Tom Wolfe memorably termed the "Me Decade"—a tidal wave of navel-gazing, self-gratification, and attention craving that these two authors attributed to very different causes.

Lasch saw narcissism as a defensive reaction to social change and instability—looking out for number one in a hostile, threatening world. In his 1979 book, *The Culture of Narcissism,* he argued that a cynical "ethic of self-preservation and psychic survival" had come to afflict America—a symptom of a country grappling with defeat in Vietnam, a growing mood of pessimism, a mass media culture centered on celebrity and fame, and centrifugal forces that were shrinking the role families played in the transmission of culture.

The narcissistic patient who had become increasingly emblematic of this self-absorbed age, Lasch wrote, often experienced "intense feelings of rage," "a sense of inner emptiness," "fantasies of omnipotence and a strong belief in [his] right to exploit others"; such a patient may be "chaotic and impulse-ridden," "ravenous for admiration but contemptuous of those he manipulates into providing it," and inclined to conform "to social rules more out of fear of punishment than from a sense of guilt."

In contrast to Lasch, Tom Wolfe saw the explosion of "Me . . . Me . . . Me" in the 1970s as an altogether happier, more hedonistic development—an act of class liberation, powered by the postwar economic boom, which had left the working and middle classes with the leisure time and disposable income to pursue the sorts of vain activities once confined to aristocrats—the "remaking, remodeling, elevating, and polishing" of one's own glorious self.

Economic times would grow considerably darker in the twenty-first century, but the self-absorption that Wolfe and Lasch described would remain a lasting feature of Western life, from the "Me Decade" of the 1970s on through the "selfie" age of Kim and

Kanye. Social media would further accelerate the ascendance of what the Columbia Law School professor Tim Wu described as "the preening self" and the urge to "capture the attention of others with the spectacle of one's self."

With this embrace of subjectivity came the diminution of objective truth: the celebration of opinion over knowledge, feelings over facts—a development that both reflected and helped foster the rise of Trump.

Three examples. Number 1: Trump, who has been accused of greatly inflating his wealth, was asked about his net worth in a 2007 court deposition. His answer, it depends: "My net worth fluctuates, and it goes up and down with markets and with attitudes and with feelings, even my own feelings." He added that it varied depending on his "general attitude at the time that the question may be asked."

Number 2: Asked whether he'd questioned Vladimir Putin about Russian interference in the election, Trump replied, "I believe that he feels that he and Russia did not meddle in the election."

Number 3: During the Republican National Convention in 2016, the CNN anchor Alisyn Camerota asked Newt Gingrich about Trump's dark, nativist law-and-order speech, which inaccurately depicted America as a country beset by violence and crime, and she was sharply rebutted by the former Speaker of the House. "I understand your view," Gingrich said. "The current view is that liberals have a whole set of statistics which theoretically may be right, but it's not where human beings are. People are frightened. People feel that their government has abandoned them."

Camerota pointed out that the crime statistics weren't liberal numbers; they came from the FBI.

The following exchange took place:

GINGRICH: No, but what I said is equally true. People feel it.

CAMEROTA: They feel it, yes, but the facts don't support it.

GINGRICH: As a political candidate, I'll go with how people feel and I'll let you go with the theoreticians.

THE TENDENCY OF Americans to focus, myopically, on their self-pursuits—sometimes to the neglect of their civic responsibilities—is not exactly new. In *Democracy in America*, written more than a century and a half before people started using Facebook and Instagram to post selfies and the internet was sorting us into silos of like-minded souls, Alexis de Tocqueville noted Americans' tendency to withdraw into "small private societies, united together by similitude of conditions, habits, and customs," in order "to indulge themselves in the enjoyments of private life." He worried that this self-absorption would diminish a sense of duty to the larger community, opening the way for a kind of soft despotism on the part of the nation's rulers—power that does not tyrannize, but "compresses, enervates, extinguishes, and stupefies a people" to the point where they are "reduced to nothing better than a flock of timid and industrious animals, of which the government is the shepherd." This was one possible cost of a materialistic society, he predicted, where people become so focused on procuring "the petty and paltry pleasures with which they glut their lives" that they neglect their responsibilities as citizens; it was difficult to conceive, he wrote, how such people who "have entirely given up the habit of self-government should succeed in making a proper choice of those by whom they are to be governed."

In the mid-twentieth century, the pursuit of self-fulfillment exploded within both the counterculture and the establishment. Predating Esalen and EST and the encounter groups that attracted hippies and New Age seekers intent on expanding their consciousness in the 1960s and 1970s were two influential figures whose doctrines of self-realization were more materialistic and more attractive to politicians and suburban Rotarians. Norman Vincent Peale, the author of the 1952 self-help bestseller *The Power of Positive Thinking*—known as "God's salesman" for his hawking of the prosperity gospel—was admired by Trump's father, Fred, and the younger Trump would internalize the celebrity pastor's teachings on self-fulfillment and the power of the mind to create its own reality. "Any fact facing us, however difficult, even seemingly hopeless, is not so important as our attitude toward that fact," Peale wrote, seeming to promote the doctrine of denial along with the doctrine of success. "A confident and optimistic thought pattern can modify or overcome the fact altogether."

Ayn Rand, also admired by Trump (over the years, *The Fountainhead* is one of the few novels he's cited as a favorite), won the fealty of several generations of politicians (including Paul Ryan, Rand Paul, Ron Paul, and Clarence Thomas) with her transactional view of the world, her equation of success and virtue, and her proud embrace of unfettered capitalism. Her argument that selfishness is a moral imperative, that man's "highest moral purpose" is "the pursuit of his own happiness," would resonate with Trump's own zero-sum view of the world and his untrammeled narcissism.

As the west lurched through the cultural upheavals of the 1960s and 1970s and their aftermath, artists struggled with how to depict this fragmenting reality. Some writers like John Barth, Donald Barthelme, and William Gass created self-conscious, postmodernist fictions that put more emphasis on form and language than on conventional storytelling. Others adopted a minimalistic approach, writing pared-down, narrowly focused stories emulating the fierce concision of Raymond Carver. And as the pursuit of broader truths became more and more unfashionable in academia, and as daily life came to feel increasingly unmoored, some writers chose to focus on the smallest, most personal truths: they wrote about themselves.

American reality had become so confounding, Philip Roth wrote in a 1961 essay (1961!), that it felt like "a kind of embarrassment to one's own meager imagination." This had resulted, he wrote, in the "voluntary withdrawal of interest by the writer of fiction from some of the grander social and political phenomena of our times," and the retreat, in his own case, to the more knowable world of the self.

In a controversial 1989 essay, Tom Wolfe lamented these developments, mourning what he saw as the demise of old-fashioned realism in American fiction, and he urged novelists to "head out into this wild, bizarre, unpredictable, Hog-stomping Baroque country of ours and reclaim it as literary property." He tried this himself in novels like *The Bonfire of the Vanities* and *A Man in Full*, using his skills as a reporter to help flesh out a spectrum of subcultures with Balzacian detail. But while Wolfe had been an influential advocate in the 1970s of the New Journalism (which put a new emphasis on the voice and point of view of the reporter), his new manifesto didn't win that many converts in the literary world. Instead, writers as disparate as Louise Erdrich, David Mitchell, Don DeLillo, Julian Barnes, Chuck Palahniuk, Gillian Flynn, and Lauren Groff would play with devices (like multiple points of view, unreliable narrators, and intertwining story lines) pioneered decades ago by innovators like Faulkner, Woolf, Ford Madox Ford, and Nabokov to try to capture the new Rashomon-like reality in which subjectivity rules and, in the infamous words of former president Bill Clinton, truth "depends on what the meaning of the word 'is' is."

But what Roth called "the sheer fact of self, the vision of self as inviolable, powerful, and nervy, self as the only real thing in an unreal environment," would remain more comfortable territory for many writers. In fact, it would lead, at the turn of the millennium, to a remarkable flowering of memoir writing, including such classics as Mary Karr's *The Liars' Club* and Dave Eggers's *A Heartbreaking Work of Staggering Genius*—works that established their authors as among the foremost voices of their generation.

The memoir boom and the popularity of blogging at the turn of the millennium would eventually culminate in Karl Ove Knausgaard's six-volume autobiographical novel—filled with minutely detailed descriptions, drawn from the author's own daily life. Along the way, there were also a lot of self-indulgent, self-dramatizing works by other authors that would have been better left in writers' private journals or social media accounts. The reductio ad absurdum of this navel-gazing was James Frey's bestselling book *A Million Little Pieces*, which was sold as a memoir but which the Smoking Gun website reported in January 2006 contained "wholly fabricated or wildly embellished details of his purported criminal career, jail terms and status as an outlaw 'wanted in three states.'" Frey, who seems to have engaged in this act of self-dramatization to make himself out to be a more notorious figure than he actually was (presumably so his subsequent "redemption" would be all the more impressive as an archetypal tale of recovery), later conceded that "most of what" the Smoking Gun site reported "was pretty accurate." For some readers, angry that they had been sold a false bill of goods, Frey's book was a con job, a repudiation of the very qualities—honesty, authenticity, candor—that memoirs are supposed to embody, but other readers shrugged off the differentiation between fact and fiction: their response a symptom of just how comfortable people had become with the blurred lines of truth.

PERSONAL TESTIMONY also became fashionable on college campuses, as the concept of objective truth fell out of favor and empirical evidence gathered by traditional research came to be regarded with suspicion. Academic writers began prefacing scholarly papers with disquisitions on their own "positioning"—their race, religion, gender, background, personal experiences that might inform or skew or ratify their analysis. Some proponents of the new "moi criticism" began writing full-fledged academic autobiographies, Adam Begley reported in *Lingua Franca* in 1994, noting that the trend toward autobiography traced back to the 1960s, to early feminist consciousness-raising groups, and that it often "spread in tandem with multiculturalism: News about minority experience often comes packaged in the first person singular. Ditto for gay studies and queer theory."

In her 1996 book, *Dedication to Hunger: The Anorexic Aesthetic in Modern Culture,* the scholar Leslie Heywood used events from her own life (like her own anorexia and a humiliating relationship with a married man) to draw analogies between anorexia and modernism, an approach that had the effect of reducing great masterpieces like T. S. Eliot's *The Waste Land* into case studies in an anti-women, anti-fat aesthetic.

Personal stories or agendas started turning up in biographies, too. No longer were biographies simple chronicles of other people's lives. Instead, they became platforms for philosophical manifestos (Norman Mailer's *Portrait of Picasso as a Young Man*), feminist polemics (Francine du Plessix Gray's *Rage and Fire,* a portrait of Flaubert's mistress Louise Colet), and deconstructionist exercises (S. Paige Baty's *American Monroe: The Making of a Body Politic*).

Arguably the most preposterous exercise in biographical writing was *Dutch: A Memoir of Ronald Reagan,* a 1999 book by Reagan's official biographer, Edmund Morris, which turned out to be a perplexing *Ragtime*-esque mashup of fact and fantasy, featuring a fictional narrator who is twenty-eight years older than the real Morris and who was supposedly saved from drowning in his youth by the future president. Instead of using his extraordinary access to a sitting president and his personal papers to create a detailed portrait of the fortieth president (or to grapple with important issues like Iran-Contra or the end of the Cold War), Morris gave readers cheesy descriptions of his fictional narrator and his fictional family and his fictional or semi-fictional hopes and dreams. Morris took this approach, he explained, because he realized he didn't "understand the first thing" about his subject—an abdication of the biographer's most basic duty—and because of his own artistic aspirations. "I want to make literature out of Ronald Reagan," he declared. He also described his use of a fictionalized narrator as "an advance in biographical honesty," a reminder to the reader of the subjective element involved in all writing.

This was an argument that echoed the self-serving reasoning of Janet Malcolm, who suggested in *The Silent Woman,* her highly partisan 1994 book about Sylvia Plath and Ted Hughes, that all biographers share her own disdain for fairness and objectivity—a disingenuous assertion, given that she made no effort to carefully weigh or evaluate material in her book but instead wrote a kind of long fan letter to Hughes, extolling his literary gifts, his physical attractiveness, his "helpless honesty." She wrote about her "feeling of tenderness toward Hughes," and how reading one of his letters, she felt her "identification with its typing swell into a feeling of intense sympathy and affection for the writer."

THE POSTMODERNIST argument that all truths are partial (and a function of one's perspective) led to the related argument that there are many legitimate ways to understand or represent an event. This both encouraged a more egalitarian discourse and made it possible for the voices of the previously disenfranchised to be heard. But it's also been exploited by those who want to make the case for offensive or debunked theories, or who want to equate things that cannot be equated. Creationists, for instance, called for teaching "intelligent design" alongside evolution in schools. "Teach both," some argued. Others said, "Teach the controversy."

A variation on this "both sides" argument was employed by President Trump when he tried to equate people demonstrating against white supremacy with the neo-Nazis who had converged in Charlottesville, Virginia, to protest the removal of Confederate statues. There were "some very fine people on both sides," Trump declared. He also said, "We condemn in the strongest possible terms this egregious display of hatred, bigotry and violence on many sides, on many sides."

Climate deniers, anti-vaxxers, and other groups who don't have science on their side bandy about phrases that wouldn't be out of place in a college class on deconstruction—phrases like "many sides," "different perspectives," "uncertainties," "multiple ways of knowing." As Naomi Oreskes and Erik M. Conway demonstrated in their 2010 book, *Merchants of Doubt*, right-wing think tanks, the fossil fuel industry, and other corporate interests that are intent on discrediting science (be it the reality of climate change or the hazards of asbestos or secondhand smoke or acid rain) have employed a strategy that was first used by the tobacco industry to try to confuse the public about the dangers of smoking. "Doubt is our product," read an infamous memo written by a tobacco industry executive in 1969, "since it is the best means of competing with the 'body of fact' that exists in the minds of the general public."

The strategy, essentially, was this: dig up a handful of so-called professionals to refute established science or argue that more research is needed; turn these false arguments into talking points and repeat them over and over; and assail the reputations of the genuine scientists on the other side. If this sounds familiar, that's because it's a tactic that's been used by Trump and his Republican allies to defend policies (on matters ranging from gun control to building a border wall) that run counter to both expert evaluation and national polls.

What Oreskes and Conway call the "Tobacco Strategy" got an assist, they argued, from elements in the mainstream media that tended "to give minority views more credence than they deserve." This false equivalence was the result of journalists confusing balance with truth telling, willful neutrality with accuracy; caving to pressure from right-wing interest groups to present "both sides"; and the format of television news shows that feature debates between opposing viewpoints—even when one side represents an overwhelming consensus and the other is an almost complete outlier in the scientific community. For instance, a 2011 BBC Trust report found that the broadcast network's science coverage paid "undue attention to marginal opinion" on the subject of man-made climate change. Or, as a headline in *The Telegraph* put it, "BBC Staff Told to Stop Inviting Cranks on to Science Programmes."

In a speech on press freedom, Christiane Amanpour addressed this issue in the context of media coverage of the 2016 presidential race, saying,

Like many people watching where I was overseas, I admit I was shocked by the exceptionally high bar put before one candidate and the exceptionally low bar put before the other candidate. It appeared much of the media got itself into knots trying to differentiate between balance, objectivity, neutrality, and crucially, truth.

We cannot continue the old paradigm—let's say like over global warming, where 99.9 percent of the empirical scientific evidence is given equal play with the tiny minority of deniers.

I learned long ago, covering the ethnic cleansing and genocide in Bosnia, never to equate victim with aggressor, never to create a false moral or factual equivalence, because then you are an accomplice to the most unspeakable crimes and consequences.

I believe in being truthful, not neutral. And I believe we must stop banalizing the truth.

4

THE VANISHING OF REALITY

Do I want to interfere with the reality tape?
   And if so, why?
Because, he thought, if I control that, I control
   reality.
      —PHILIP K. DICK, "THE ELECTRIC ANT"

SURREAL" AND "CHAOS" HAVE BECOME two of those words invoked hourly by journalists trying to describe daily reality in America in the second decade of the new millennium, at a time when nineteen kids are shot every day in the United States, when the president of the United States plays a game of nuclear chicken with North Korea's Kim Jong-un, when artificial intelligence engines are writing poetry and novellas, when it's getting more and more difficult to tell the difference between headlines from *The Onion* and headlines from CNN.

Trump's unhinged presidency represents some sort

of climax in the warping of reality, but the burgeoning disorientation people have been feeling over the disjuncture between what they know to be true and what they are told by politicians, between common sense and the workings of the world, traces back to the 1960s, when society began fragmenting and official narratives—purveyed by the government, by the establishment, by elites—started to break down and the news cycle started to speed up. In 1961, Philip Roth wrote of American reality, "It stupefies, it sickens, it infuriates." The daily newspapers, he complained, "fill one with wonder and awe: is it possible? is it happening? And of course with sickness and despair. The fixes, the scandals, the insanities, the treacheries, the idiocies, the lies, the pieties, the noise . . ."

Roth's sense that actuality was exceeding fiction writers' imagination (and throwing up real-life figures like Richard Nixon and Roy Cohn who were the envy of any novelist) would be echoed more than half a century later by writers of satire and spy thrillers in the Trump era. And his observation that novelists were having difficulty dealing imaginatively with a world they felt to be confounding helps explain why journalism—particularly what Tom Wolfe called the New Journalism—began eclipsing fiction in capturing what life was like in the 1960s, as the *Esquire* anthology aptly titled *Smiling Through the Apocalypse* (featuring classic magazine pieces by such writers as Norman Mailer, Michael Herr, and Gay Talese) attested.

POLITICIANS HAD always spun reality, but television—and later the internet—gave them new platforms on which to prevaricate. When the Republican strategist Lee Atwater observed in the 1980s that "perception is reality," he was bluntly articulating an insight about human psychology that Homer well knew when he immortalized Odysseus as a wily trickster, adept at deception and disguise. But Atwater's cold-blooded use of that precept in using wedge issues to advance the GOP's southern strategy— and to create the infamous Willie Horton ad in the 1988 presidential campaign—injected mainstream American politics with an alarming strain of win-at-all-costs Machiavellianism using mass media as a delivery system.

Nearly three decades later, Trump would cast immigrants in the role of Willie Horton, and turning the clock back further, he would exchange dog-whistle racism for the more overt racism and rhetoric of George Wallace. At the same time, he instinctively grasped that the new internet-driven landscape and voters' growing ignorance about issues made it easier than ever to play to voters' fears and resentments by promoting sticky, viral narratives that served up alternate realities. He also amped up efforts to discredit journalism as "fake news," attacking reporters as "enemies of the people"—a chilling term once used by Lenin and Stalin.

It wasn't just that Trump lied reflexively and shamelessly, but that those hundreds upon hundreds of lies came together to create equally false story lines that appealed to people's fears. Depicting America as a country reeling from crime (when, in fact, the crime rate was experiencing historic lows—less than half what it was at its peak in 1991). A country beset by waves of violent immigrants (when, in fact, studies show that immigrants are less likely to commit violent crimes than U.S.-born citizens). Immigrants who are a burden to the country and who should be vetted more carefully (when, in fact, thirty-one of seventy-eight American Nobel Prizes since 2000 were won by immigrants, and immigrants and their kids have helped found an estimated 60 percent of the top U.S. tech companies, worth nearly four trillion dollars). In short, Trump argued, a nation in deep trouble and in need of a savior.

Long before he entered politics, Trump was using lies as a business tool. He claimed that his flagship building, Trump Tower, is sixty-eight floors high, when, in fact, it's only fifty-eight floors high. He also pretended to be a PR man named John Barron or John Miller to create a sock puppet who could boast about his—Trump's—achievements. He lied to puff himself up, to generate business under false pretenses, and to play to people's expectations. Everything was purely transactional; all that mattered was making the sale.

He spent years as a real-estate developer and reality-TV star, promiscuously branding himself (Trump Hotels, Trump Menswear, Trump Natural Spring Water, Trump University, Trump Steaks, Trump Vodka, Trump Home Collection), and like most successful advertisers—and successful propagandists—he understood that the frequent repetition of easy-to-remember and simplistic taglines worked to embed merchandise (and his name) in potential customers' minds. Decades before handing out "MAGA" hats at his rallies, he'd become an expert at staging what the historian Daniel Boorstin called "pseudo-events"—that is, events "planned, planted, or incited" primarily "for the immediate purpose of being reported or reproduced."

Boorstin's 1962 book, *The Image*—which would inform the work of myriad writers from French theorists like Baudrillard and Guy Debord, to social critics like Neil Postman and Douglas Rushkoff—uncannily foresaw reality TV decades before the Kardashians or the Osbournes or any number of desperate housewives actually showed up in our living rooms. For that matter, he anticipated the rise of someone very much like Donald J. Trump: a celebrity known, in Boorstin's words, for his "well-knownness" (and who would even host a show called *The Celebrity Apprentice*).

Boorstin's descriptions of the nineteenth-century impresario and circus showman P. T. Barnum—who ran a New York City museum of curiosities filled with hoaxes like a mermaid (which turned out to be the remains of a monkey stitched together with the tail of a fish)—will sound uncannily familiar to contemporary readers: a self-proclaimed "prince of humbugs" whose "great discovery was not how easy it was to deceive the public but rather how much the public enjoyed being deceived" as long as it was being entertained.

Much the way images were replacing ideals, Boorstin wrote in *The Image,* the idea of "credibility" was replacing the idea of truth. People were less interested in whether something was a fact than in whether it was "convenient that it should be believed." And as verisimilitude replaced truth as a measurement, "the socially rewarded art" became "that of making things seem true"; no wonder that the new masters of the universe in the early 1960s were the Mad Men of Madison Avenue.

BAUDRILLARD WOULD take such observations further, suggesting that in today's media-centric culture people have come to prefer the "hyperreal"—that is, simulated or fabricated realities like Disneyland—to the boring, everyday "desert of the real."

Artists like Jorge Luis Borges, William Gibson, Stanislaw Lem, Philip K. Dick, and Federico Fellini grappled with similar themes, creating stories in which the borders between the real and the virtual, the actual and the imagined, the human and the posthuman blur, overlap, even collapse. In the story "Tlön, Uqbar, Orbis Tertius," Borges describes "a secret society of astronomers, biologists, engineers, metaphysicians, poets, chemists, mathematicians, moralists, painters and geometricians" who invent an unknown planet named Tlön: they conjure its geography, its architecture, its systems of thinking. Bits and pieces of

Tlön start surfacing in the real world: an artifact here, a description there, and things speed up around 1942; eventually, the narrator notes, the teachings of Tlön have spread so widely that the history he learned as a child has been obliterated and replaced by "a fictitious past."

Borges drew direct parallels between the power of fictions about Tlön to insinuate themselves into human consciousness and the power of deadly political ideologies based on lies to infect entire nations; both, he suggested, provide internally consistent narratives that appeal to people hungering to make sense of the world. "Reality gave ground on more than one point," Borges wrote. "The truth is that it hankered to give ground. Ten years ago, any symmetrical system whatsoever which gave the appearance of order—dialectical materialism, anti-Semitism, Nazism—was enough to fascinate men. Why not fall under the spell of Tlön and submit to the minute and vast evidence of an ordered planet? Useless to reply that reality, too, is ordered. It may be so, but in accordance with divine laws—I translate: inhuman laws—which we will never completely perceive. Tlön may be a labyrinth, but it is a labyrinth plotted by men, a labyrinth destined to be deciphered by men."

Thomas Pynchon's novels explore similar themes—

more relevant than ever in a world suffering from information overload. Reeling from a kind of spiritual vertigo, his characters wonder whether the paranoiacs have it right—that there are malign conspiracies and hidden agendas connecting all the dots. Or whether the nihilists are onto something—that there is no signal in the noise, only chaos and randomness. "If there is something comforting—religious, if you want—about paranoia," he wrote in *Gravity's Rainbow*, "there is still also anti-paranoia, where nothing is connected to anything, a condition not many of us can bear for long."

IN A 2016 documentary titled *HyperNormalisation*, the British filmmaker Adam Curtis created an expressionistic, montage-driven meditation on life in the post-truth era; the title (which also seems to allude to Baudrillard) was taken from a term coined by the anthropologist Alexei Yurchak to describe life in the final years of the Soviet Union, when people both understood the absurdity of the propaganda the government had been selling them for decades and had difficulty envisioning any alternative. In *HyperNormalisation*, which was released shortly before the 2016 U.S. election on the BBC's iPlayer platform,

Curtis says in voice-over narration that people in the West had also stopped believing the stories politicians had been telling them for years, and Trump realized that "in the face of that, you could play with reality" and in the process "further undermine and weaken the old forms of power."

Some Trump allies on the far right also seek to redefine reality on their own terms. Invoking the iconography of the movie *The Matrix*—in which the hero is given a choice between two pills, a red one (representing knowledge and the harsh truths of reality) and a blue one (representing soporific illusion and denial)—members of the alt-right and some aggrieved men's rights groups talk about "red-pilling the normies," which means converting people to their cause. In other words, selling their inside-out alternative reality, in which white people are suffering from persecution, multiculturalism poses a grave threat, and men have been oppressed by women.

Alice Marwick and Rebecca Lewis, the authors of a study on online disinformation, argue that "once groups have been red-pilled on one issue, they're likely to be open to other extremist ideas. Online cultures that used to be relatively nonpolitical are beginning to seethe with racially charged anger. Some sci-fi, fandom, and gaming communities—having

accepted run-of-the-mill anti-feminism—are beginning to espouse white-nationalist ideas. 'Ironic' Nazi
iconography and hateful epithets are becoming serious expressions of anti-Semitism."

One of the tactics used by the alt-right to spread
its ideas online, Marwick and Lewis argue, is to ini-
tially dilute more extreme views as gateway ideas to
court a wider audience; among some groups of young
men, they write, "it's a surprisingly short leap from
rejecting political correctness to blaming women, immigrants, or Muslims for their problems."

Many misogynist and white supremacist memes,
in addition to a lot of fake news like Pizzagate, origi-
nate or gain initial momentum on sites like 4chan
and Reddit—before accumulating enough buzz to
make the leap to Facebook and Twitter, where they
can attract more mainstream attention. Renee Di-
Resta, who studies conspiracy theories on the web,
argues that Reddit can be a useful testing ground
for bad actors—including foreign governments like
Russia—to try out memes or fake stories to see how
much traction they get.

DiResta warned in the spring of 2016 that the
algorithms of social networks—which give people
news that's popular and trending, rather than accurate or important—are helping to promote conspiracy

theories. This sort of fringe content can both affect how people think and seep into public policy debates on matters like vaccines, zoning laws, and water fluoridation. Part of the problem is an "asymmetry of passion" on social media: while most people won't devote hours to writing posts that reinforce the obvious, DiResta says, "passionate truthers and extremists produce copious amounts of content in their commitment to 'wake up the sheeple.'"

Recommendation engines, she adds, help connect conspiracy theorists with one another to the point that "we are long past merely partisan filter bubbles and well into the realm of siloed communities that experience their own reality and operate with their own facts." At this point, she concludes, "the Internet doesn't just reflect reality anymore; it shapes it."

5

THE CO-OPTING OF LANGUAGE

Without clear language, there is no standard of truth.

—John le Carré

LANGUAGE IS TO HUMANS, THE WRITER James Carroll once observed, what water is to fish: "We swim in language. We think in language. We live in language." This is why Orwell wrote that "political chaos is connected with the decay of language," divorcing words from meaning and opening up a chasm between a leader's real and declared aims. This is why America and the world feel so disoriented by the stream of lies issued by the Trump White House and the president's use of language as a tool to disseminate distrust and discord. And this is why authoritarian regimes throughout history have co-opted everyday language in an effort to control not just how people communicate but also how they think—exactly the way the Ministry of Truth in Orwell's *1984* aims to deny the existence of external reality and safeguard Big Brother's infallibility.

Orwell's "Newspeak" is a fictional language, but it often mirrors and satirizes the "wooden language" imposed by Communist authorities in the Soviet Union and eastern Europe. Among the characteristics of "wooden language" that the French scholar Françoise Thom identified in a 1987 thesis (*La langue de bois*) were abstraction and the avoidance of the concrete; tautologies ("the theories of Marx are true because they are correct"); bad metaphors ("the fascist octopus has sung its swan song"); and Manichaeanism that divides the world into things good and things evil (and nothing in between).

Mao's Communist Party also adopted a plan of linguistic engineering soon after taking power in China in 1949, creating a new political vocabulary: some words were suppressed; others were injected with new meanings; and party slogans were drummed into people's brains through constant repetition. People were made to understand that there were "correct" and "incorrect" ways to speak, whether it was delivering a work report or engaging in a required round of self-criticism.

One of history's most detailed accounts of how

totalitarianism affects everyday language was written by Victor Klemperer, a German-Jewish linguist who survived World War II in Dresden. Klemperer kept a remarkable set of diaries chronicling life under Nazi rule in Germany (*I Will Bear Witness*), and he also wrote a study (*The Language of the Third Reich*) about how the Nazis used words as "tiny doses of arsenic" to poison and subvert the German culture from within. The book is a harrowing case study in how the Reich "permeated the flesh and blood of the people" through idioms and sentence structures that were "imposed on them in a million repetitions and taken on board mechanically and unconsciously." It's also a cautionary tale, every bit as unnerving as Orwell's *1984,* to other countries and future generations about how swiftly and insidiously an autocrat can weaponize language to suppress critical thinking, inflame bigotry, and hijack a democracy.

Klemperer didn't think Hitler compared with Mussolini as a speaker, and he was surprised that the Nazi leader—whom he saw as an angry, insecure man with an annoying voice and a propensity to bellow—amassed such a following. He attributed Hitler's success less to his heinous ideology than to his skills at going around other politicians to reach out directly to the people—the word *Volk* was regularly invoked, and

Hitler portrayed himself as their voice, their messiah. The big spectacles (effectively pseudo-events) that he and Goebbels staged were a help. "The splendour of the banners, parades, garlands, fanfares and choruses" that surrounded Hitler's speeches, Klemperer notes, served as an effective "advertising ploy" that conflated the führer with the grandeur of the state.

As in the Soviet Union and Maoist China, words underwent a sinister metamorphosis in Nazi Germany. The word *fanatisch* (fanatical), Klemperer wrote, went from denoting "a threatening and repulsive quality" associated with bloodlust and cruelty to being an "inordinately complimentary epithet," evoking the qualities of devotion and courage needed to fuel the Reich. The word *kämpferisch* (aggressive, belligerent) also became a word of praise, meaning admirable "self-assertion through defense or attack." Meanwhile, the word "system" was scorned, because it was associated with the Weimar Republic, which the Nazis despised in much the same way that right-wing Republicans today despise what they call the deep state.

Hitler's *Mein Kampf* was published in 1925, and Klemperer notes that the book "literally fixed the essential features" of Nazi oratory and prose. In 1933, this "language of a clique became the language of the people." It would be as if, say, the argot of the alt-right—its coded use of language to identify fellow travelers; its racial and misogynist slurs—were to be completely mainstreamed and made a part of routine political and social discourse.

Klemperer devoted an entire chapter to the Nazis' obsession with numbers and superlatives; everything had to be the best or the most. If a German from the Third Reich went on an elephant hunt, Klemperer wrote, he would have to boast that he'd "finished off the biggest elephants in the world, in unimaginable numbers, with the best weapon on earth." Many of the Nazis' own numbers (regarding enemy soldiers killed, prisoners taken, audience numbers for a radio broadcast of a rally) were so exaggerated that they took on what Klemperer calls a "fairy-tale quality." In 1942, he writes, "Hitler says in the Reichstag that Napoleon fought in Russia in temperatures of minus 25 degrees, but that he, Commanding Officer Hitler, had fought at minus 45, even at minus 52." All the lying and hyperbole eventually reached the point, Klemperer continues, that it became "meaningless and utterly ineffective, finally bringing about a belief in the very opposite of what it intended."

———

TRUMP'S MENDACITY is so extreme that news organizations have resorted to assembling lengthy lists of lies he's told, insults he's delivered, norms he's violated, in addition to hiring squads of fact-checkers. And his shamelessness has emboldened politicians around him to lie with even more effrontery than ever. Republicans in Congress, for instance, blatantly lied about the effects their tax bill would have on the deficit and social safety net provisions, just as they lied about how much it would help the middle class, when in fact it was all about giving tax breaks to corporations and the very rich.

Trump's assault on language is not confined to his torrent of lies, but extends to his taking of words and principles intrinsic to the rule of law and contaminating them with personal agendas and political partisanship. In doing so, he's exchanged the language of democracy and its ideals for the language of autocracy. He demands allegiance not to the U.S. Constitution but to himself, and he expects members of Congress and the judiciary to applaud his policies and wishes, regardless of what they think best serves the interests of the American people.

With other phrases, Trump has performed the disturbing Orwellian trick ("WAR IS PEACE," "FREEDOM IS SLAVERY," "IGNORANCE IS

STRENGTH") of using words to mean the exact opposite of what they really mean. It's not just his taking the term "fake news," turning it inside out, and using it to try to discredit journalism that he finds threatening or unflattering. He's also called the investigation into Russian election interference "the single greatest witch hunt in American political history," when he is the one who has repeatedly attacked the press, the Justice Department, the FBI, the intelligence services, any institution he regards as hostile.

In fact, Trump has the perverse habit of accusing opponents of the very sins he is guilty of himself: "Lyin' Ted," "Crooked Hillary," "Crazy Bernie." He accused Clinton of being "a bigot who sees people of color only as votes, not as human beings worthy of a better future," and he has asserted that "there was tremendous collusion on behalf of the Russians and the Democrats."

In Orwell's language of Newspeak in *1984*, a word like "blackwhite" has "two mutually contradictory meanings": "Applied to an opponent, it means the habit of impudently claiming that black is white, in contradiction of the plain facts. Applied to a Party member, it means a loyal willingness to say that black is white when Party discipline demands this."

This, too, has an unnerving echo in the behavior of

Trump White House officials and Republican members of Congress who lie on the president's behalf and routinely make pronouncements that flout the evidence in front of people's eyes. The administration, in fact, debuted with the White House press secretary, Sean Spicer, insisting that Trump's inaugural crowds were the "largest audience" ever—an assertion that defied photographic evidence and was rated by Politi-Fact a "Pants on Fire" lie.

These sorts of lies, the journalist Masha Gessen has pointed out, are told for the same reason that Vladimir Putin lies: "to assert power over truth itself." In the case of Ukraine, Gessen wrote in late 2016, "Putin insisted on lying in the face of clear and convincing evidence to the contrary, and in each case his subsequent shift to truthful statements were not admissions given under duress: they were proud, even boastful affirmatives made at his convenience. Together, they communicated a single message: Putin's power lies in being able to say what he wants, when he wants, regardless of the facts. He is president of his country and king of reality."

In *1984*, another way the party and Big Brother exert control over reality is by adjusting the past to conform with their worldview: "It is not merely that speeches, statistics and records of every kind must be constantly brought up to date in order to show that the predictions of the Party were in all cases right. It is also that no change in doctrine or in political alignment can ever be admitted. For to change one's mind, or even one's policy, is a confession of weakness. If, for example, Eurasia or Eastasia (whichever it may be) is the enemy today, then that country must always have been the enemy. And if the facts say otherwise, then the facts must be altered. Thus history is continuously rewritten."

Consider this: within days of Trump's inauguration, changes were being made to the climate change pages on the White House website. Meanwhile, environmentalists were frantically trying to download and archive government climate data—worried that it might be destroyed or lost or hidden by a hostile administration. Some of their fears were realized later in 2017, when the EPA announced that its website was "undergoing changes that reflect the agency's new direction," including this Orwellian phrase: "updating language to reflect the approach of new leadership."

On educational pages controlled by the Department of Energy, phrases about renewable energy were switched to ones advocating the use of fossil fuels, and links to the Obama administration's 2013 climate report and references to UN meetings on climate change vanished from State Department pages.

USDA employees were informed that their social media posts should be reviewed by administrators "to remove references to policy priorities and initiatives of the previous Administration." And after the National Park Service retweeted a post showing aerial photographs that compared the size of Trump's inaugural crowds with those of President Obama's, the agency's digital team was told to temporarily suspend its use of Twitter. That retweet was soon deleted.

AT THE same time, Trump continued his personal assault on the English language. Trump's incoherence (his twisted syntax, his reversals, his insincerity, his bad faith, and his inflammatory bombast) is both emblematic of the chaos he creates and thrives on as well as an essential instrument in his liar's tool kit. His interviews, off-teleprompter speeches, and tweets are a startling jumble of insults, exclamations, boasts, digressions, non sequiturs, qualifications, exhortations, and innuendos—a bully's efforts to intimidate, gaslight, polarize, and scapegoat.

Precise words, like facts, mean little to Trump, as interpreters, who struggle to translate his grammatical anarchy, can attest. Chuck Todd, the anchor of NBC's *Meet the Press*, observed that after several of his appearances as a candidate Trump would lean back in his chair and ask the control booth to replay his segment on a monitor—without sound: "He wants to see what it all looked like. He will watch the whole thing on mute."

He is equally nonchalant about spelling. There was the famous "covfefe" tweet: "Despite the constant negative press covfefe." And his description of the Chinese seizure of a U.S. Navy drone as an "unpresidented act." He also tweeted that he was "honered to serve you, the great American People, as your 45th President of the United States!" Twitter typos are common, of course, and they are hardly the most alarming aspect of Trump's compulsion to tweet. But they are indicative of his impulsive, live-in-the-moment, can't-think-about-the-fallout posture. And his typos are contagious. The White House released a statement about a presidential trip to Israel, saying that one of his goals was to "promote the possibility of lasting peach." Other White House releases misspelled the name of Jon Huntsman Jr., Trump's nominee to be ambassador to Russia, and misspelled the name of the British prime minister, Theresa May. The official inauguration poster read, "No dream is too big, no challenge is to great." And tickets for his first State of the Union address (which had to be reprinted) read, "Address to Congress on the State of the Uniom." Harmless enough glitches, perhaps, but indicative of the administration's larger carelessness and dysfunction—its cavalier disregard for accuracy, details, and precision.

TRUMP'S TWEETS have been deemed official pronouncements of the president of the United States and will no doubt one day be printed out, finely bound, and shelved by someone wearing white gloves in a gold-shellacked presidential library. Whether they are distractions meant to divert attention from the Russia investigations, the stream-of-consciousness rants of an attention-craving narcissist, or part of a more deliberate strategy to acclimate people to the aberrant, the tweets have immediate consequences around the planet, escalating nuclear tensions with North Korea, alienating whole countries and continents, and sending tremors through the post–World War II order.

Trump's retweeting of anti-Muslim videos from the far-right group Britain First earned a sharp rebuke from the U.K.'s Theresa May and helped mainstream a heretofore marginal hate group.

His rants against journalism as "fake news" have enabled further crackdowns on press freedom in countries like Russia, China, Turkey, and Hungary where reporters already work under duress. And they have been taken as license by leaders of authoritarian regimes to dismiss reports of human rights abuses and war crimes in their own countries. After Amnesty International reported that up to thirteen thousand prisoners were killed at a military prison outside Damascus between 2011 and 2015, the Syrian president, Bashar al-Assad, said, "You can forge anything these days"—"We are living in a fake news era." And in Myanmar, where the military is carrying out a horrifying campaign of ethnic cleansing against the Rohingya, a long-persecuted Muslim minority, an officer in the state security ministry declared, "There is no such thing as Rohingya. It is fake news."

The scholar Ruth Ben-Ghiat, a professor of history and Italian studies at New York University who has drawn parallels between Trump's rise and that of Mussolini, argues that authoritarians typically test "the limits of what the public, press, and political class will tolerate" and that Trump's incendiary tweets and remarks are efforts "to see how much Americans and the GOP will let him get away with—and when, if ever, they will say 'enough.'"

A 1995 essay about Mussolini and "ur-fascism" by the Italian scholar Umberto Eco also sheds light, when read retrospectively, on Trump's language and use of authoritarian tropes. Many of the features Eco described as being intrinsic to fascism will ominously remind the reader of Trump's demagoguery: an appeal to nationalism and people's "fear of difference"; a rejection of science and rational discourse; an invocation of tradition and the past; and a proclivity for equating disagreement with treason.

More specifically, Eco wrote that "Mussolini did not have any philosophy; he had only rhetoric": it was "a fuzzy totalitarianism, a collage of different philosophical and political ideas, a beehive of contradictions." Ur-fascism employs "an impoverished vocabulary, and an elementary syntax," Eco added, "in order to limit the instruments for complex and critical reasoning." And it regards "the People" not as citizens or individuals but as "a monolithic entity expressing the Common Will," which the leader pretends to interpret; the leader puts himself forth—

instead of, say, a parliament or legislature—as "the Voice of the People." If that sounds oddly familiar, it's because Trump, in his Republican National Convention address, said to the audience, "I'm with you—the American people. I am your voice."

6

FILTERS, SILOS, AND TRIBES

We're all islands shouting lies to each other across seas of misunderstanding.

—RUDYARD KIPLING, 1890

SHORTLY BEFORE THE 2004 ELECTION, Arthur Miller—the playwright and a dedicated liberal—wondered, "How can the polls be neck and neck when I don't know one Bush supporter?"

Since then, of course, the walls of our political silos have only grown taller; the insulation of our echo chambers, that much thicker. Even before we were being sealed in impermeable filter bubbles by Facebook news feeds and Google search data, we were living in communities that had become increasingly segregated in terms of politics, culture, geography, and lifestyle. Add to that partisan news sources like Fox News, Breitbart, and Drudge, and it's no surprise that the Rashomon effect has taken hold: common ground between citizens from opposing political parties is rapidly shrinking, and the whole idea of consensus is becoming a thing of the past.

A 2016 Pew survey showed that 45 percent of Republicans view Democratic policies as a threat to the nation's well-being, and 41 percent of Democrats say the same about GOP policies. And the animosity goes well beyond policy disagreements; it's personal. Seventy percent of Democrats in that Pew survey said that Republicans are more close-minded than other Americans; meanwhile, 47 percent of Republicans said Democrats are more immoral than other Americans, and 46 percent said they are lazier.

Such partisanship is being inflated further by Russian trolls seeking to undermine democracy in America by amplifying social divisions through fake news and fake social media accounts and by President Trump's use of inflammatory remarks to pander to his base and bait his adversaries. It's telling that the old national motto *E pluribus unum* (Out of many, one) has been removed from Trump's commemorative presidential coins and replaced with his own slogan "Make America Great Again."

These growing divides in America are only a couple of decades old, according to Bill Bishop's book, *The Big*

Sort. In the 1950s, 1960s, and 1970s, Bishop wrote, communities seemed to be growing more politically integrated, and "there was an economic convergence, too," as Sunbelt prosperity spread in the South. But around 1980 or so something happened, says Bishop: people had begun reordering their lives around "their values, their tastes, and their beliefs"—in part, as a response to the social and cultural dislocations that followed in the wake of the 1960s. People with college degrees were gravitating toward cities, while rural areas slipped behind economically.

"As we've lost trust in traditional institutions," Bishop wrote, "the tenuous bonds of the workplace have proven insufficient to satisfy people's need for belonging." In response, people found a sense of community by seeking out like-minded neighborhoods, churches, social clubs, and other organizations. It's a dynamic that would be amplified at light speed by the internet—by news sites catering to particular ideological points of view, by special interest bulletin boards, and by social media that's helped people further sort themselves into silos of shared interests. By the turn of the millennium, Bishop wrote, the divisions were less about ideology than about tastes and values, but "as the parties have come to represent lifestyle—and as lifestyle has defined communities—everything seems divisible, Republican or Democratic." Everything meaning not just your views on health care or voting rights or global warming but where you shop, what you eat, what sorts of movies you watch. A 2017 Pew survey showed that Americans don't even agree about the value of a college education: while 72 percent of Democrats and Democratic-leaning independents said colleges and universities have a positive effect on the country, a majority of Republicans and Republican leaners (58 percent) have a negative view of those institutions of higher learning.

Meanwhile, the number of people in the middle— independents or swing voters—dwindled in clout, or at least in the attention they received from many politicians. In his book *The Second Civil War,* the veteran political reporter Ronald Brownstein described how George W. Bush's political advisers reviewed the data from the 2000 campaign and decided to focus in 2004 on energizing the base and encouraging turnout among Republicans—a harbinger of the play-to-the-base strategy Trump would later pursue so relentlessly. As one Bush adviser told Brownstein, "This is not designed to be a 55 percent presidency. This is designed to be a presidency that moves as much as possible of what we believe into law while holding fifty plus one of the country and the Congress." In 2016, Hillary Clinton's campaign basically wrote off the white working-class vote (the vote her husband, Bill, had owned) and focused, instead, on turning out her base.

Ideological consistency grew over the years: a 2014 Pew survey found that in the two decades after 1994 more Democrats gave "uniformly liberal responses" to policy questions (about matters like immigration, the environment, the role of government), while more Republicans gave "uniformly conservative responses." Those members of both parties with the most consistent views, the Pew study noted, had a "disproportionate influence on the political process"; they were more likely to vote, more likely to donate money, more likely to contact elected officials. And then there is gerrymandering, which has favored Republicans since they launched a concerted effort after Obama's election in 2008 to gain control of state governments, which are in charge of drawing (or redrawing) congressional districts. The new, often highly misshapen districts, drawn with the help of computer software, gave Republicans a substantial advantage in capturing and holding on to the House of Representatives, and they also tended to tilt districts further to the right, which made many elected officials reluctant to compromise with Democrats when they got to Washington, out of fear of being primaried on their right.

For many of these committed partisans, supporting their party was like being a rabid, die-hard fan of a favorite NBA, MLB, or NFL team; it was part of their own identity, and their team could do no wrong. They might hate a particular policy or a particular candidate—much the way they might blame their team's coach for a bad play, or loathe an overpaid, underperforming player received in a trade—but short of the apocalypse they were going to remain loyal fans while wishing pain and humiliation upon their opponents.

Polarized voting in Congress mirrored these developments: by 2014, a Pew report noted, Republicans and Democrats on Capitol Hill were "further apart from one another than at any point in modern history"; it also highlighted that rising polarization among elected officials was "asymmetrical, with much of the widening gap between the two parties attributable to a rightward shift among Republicans."

The chief reason for this asymmetry was the explosion of right-wing media. Back in the 1990s, Rush Limbaugh proved that incendiary invective and showmanship—two things Donald Trump would learn from him—could win him a lucrative national audience, and for decades his faithful dittoheads loyally repeated whatever he said, even when what he said was ridiculous. In one diatribe, Limbaugh asserted that "the Four Corners of Deceit are government, academia, science, and the media." He also declared that "scientists wear white lab coats and they look really official" but "they're frauds. They're bought and paid for by the left."

In the three decades since the FCC revoked the Fairness Doctrine (which required TV and radio stations to devote some of their programming to important issues of the day and air opposing views on those issues) and the two decades since Roger Ailes and Rupert Murdoch launched Fox News, right-wing media has grown into a sprawling, solipsistic network that relentlessly repeats its own tropes (the dangers of immigration, the untrustworthiness of mainstream media, the evils of big government, and so on), and it's succeeded in framing many debates in the national conversation through its sheer shamelessness and decibel level. Breitbart News, which Steve Bannon described as a "platform for the alt-right," and the Sinclair Broadcast Group, which reaches an estimated 38 percent of American households through local news broadcasts, have expanded the right-wing media universe, along with countless online sites, YouTube channels, and radio broadcasts. In an Orwellian move, Sinclair has even forced local news anchors to read a scripted message about "false news" that echoes President Trump's own rhetoric undermining real reporting.

Many of these outlets don't even go through the motions of trying to provide verifiable facts and information, but instead attempt to spin what one talk show host calls "truth-based content" into self-serving, precooked narratives that ratify audiences' existing beliefs or gin up their worst fears.

In recent years, the conservative radio host Charlie Sykes observed, conservative media created an "alternate reality bubble" that "destroyed our own immunity to fake news, while empowering the worst and most reckless on the right."

A 2017 Harvard study of more than 1.25 million stories (published online between April 1, 2015, and Election Day in November 2016) concluded that pro-Trump audiences relied heavily on this "insulated knowledge community," which uses "social media as a backbone to transmit a hyper-partisan perspective to the world" and reinforces users' shared worldview while poisoning them against mainstream journalism that might challenge their preconceptions. The result: an environment in which the president can allude to a terrorist event in Sweden that never happened, or a presidential adviser can reference a nonexistent "Bowling Green massacre."

WITH TRIBAL POLITICS increasingly dominating Republican and Democratic politics, candidates scramble to lock down their party's base during the primary process. Much of the Republican base now reacts instantly with knee-jerk denial when it comes to issues like gun violence, Obamacare, or global warming. Never mind statistics, expert analyses, carefully researched university or government studies, in some cases even their own self-interest—a lot of hard-core Trump supporters dismiss such evidence as never-to-be-trusted liberal or deep state politics. For these partisans, party loyalty and tribal politics matter more than facts, more than morality and decency: witness the Republicans who supported Senate candidate Roy Moore, who was accused of sexual misconduct against teenage girls, and the Trump supporters who booed John McCain, a genuine war hero, and viciously said God had punished him with cancer for standing up to Trump.

As the journalist Andrew Sullivan wrote, "The enduring, complicated divides of ideology, geography, party, class, religion, and race have mutated into something deeper, simpler to map, and therefore much more ominous": not simple political polarization, but the fracture of the country into "two coherent tribes, eerily balanced in political power, fighting not just to advance their own side but to provoke, condemn, and defeat the other."

Assorted theories have been advanced to explain confirmation bias—why people rush to embrace information that supports their beliefs while rejecting information that disputes them: that first impressions are difficult to dislodge, that there's a primitive instinct to defend one's turf, that people tend to have emotional rather than intellectual responses to being challenged and are loath to carefully examine evidence.

Group dynamics only exaggerate these tendencies, the author and legal scholar Cass Sunstein observed in his book *Going to Extremes*: insularity often means limited information input (and usually information that reinforces preexisting views) and a desire for peer approval; and if the group's leader "does not encourage dissent and is inclined to an identifiable conclusion, it is highly likely that the group as a whole will move toward that conclusion."

Once the group has been psychologically walled off, Sunstein wrote, "the information and views of those outside the group can be discredited, and hence nothing will disturb the process of polarization as group members continue to talk." In fact, groups of like-minded people can become breeding grounds for extreme movements. "Terrorists are made, not born," Sunstein observed, "and terrorist networks often operate in just this way. As a result, they can move otherwise ordinary people to violent acts."

Charlie Sykes decided to step down from his popular radio show at the end of 2016. Politics had become a "binary tribal world," he pointed out, in which voters "tolerate bizarre behavior, dishonesty, crudity and cruelty, because the other side is always worse." What his listeners wouldn't tolerate was his criticism of Trump or his objections that crazy conspiracy theories about Hillary Clinton and Barack Obama were demonstrably false. His listeners had become accustomed to rejecting mainstream sources of news and, for that matter, simple facts.

"In the new Right media culture," he wrote in his 2017 book, *How the Right Lost Its Mind*, "negative information simply no longer penetrates; gaffes and scandals can be snuffed out, ignored, or spun; counternarratives can be launched. Trump has proven that a candidate can be immune to the narratives, criticism, and fact-checking of the mainstream media."

LONG GONE are the pre-cable days when many people got their news from one of three TV networks and watched many of the same television shows like *All in the Family* and *The Mary Tyler Moore Show*. New *Star Wars* movies and the Super Bowl remain some of the few communal events that capture an audience cutting across demographic lines.

As for news, an increasingly fragmented media environment offers sites and publications targeted at niche audiences from the reddest red to the bluest blue. Facebook, Twitter, YouTube, and many other sites use algorithms to personalize the information you see—information customized on the basis of earlier data they've collected about you.

"With Google personalized for everyone," the internet activist Eli Pariser wrote in his book, *The Filter Bubble*, "the query 'stem cells' might produce diametrically opposed results for scientists who support stem cell research and activists who oppose it. 'Proof of climate change' might turn up different results for an environmental activist and an oil company executive. In polls, a huge majority of us assume search engines are unbiased. But that may be just because they're increasingly biased to share our own views. More and more, your computer monitor is a kind of one-way mirror, reflecting your own interests while algorithmic observers watch what you click."

Because social media sites give us information that tends to confirm our view of the world—what Pariser calls "an endless you-loop"—people live in increasingly narrow content silos and correspondingly smaller walled gardens of thought. It's a big reason why liberals and conservatives, Democrats and Republicans, find it harder and harder to agree on facts and why a shared sense of reality is becoming elusive. It also helps explain why elites in New York and Washington—including the Clinton campaign and much of the press—were so shocked by Trump's win in the 2016 election.

"If algorithms are going to curate the world for us," Pariser warned in a 2011 TED talk, "if they're going to decide what we get to see and what we don't get to see, then we need to make sure that they're not just keyed to relevance but that they also show us things that are uncomfortable or challenging or important, other points of view."

7

ATTENTION DEFICIT

When you want to know how things really work,
study them when they're coming apart.

—WILLIAM GIBSON, *ZERO HISTORY*

WHEN IT COMES TO SPREADING FAKE news and undermining belief in objectivity, technology has proven a highly flammable accelerant. Increasingly we have become aware of the dark side of what was imagined as a transformative catalyst for innovation.

Tim Berners-Lee, who drew up a proposal in 1989 for what would become the World Wide Web, envisioned a universal information system, connecting people across boundaries of language and location and sharing information that would lead to unprecedented creativity and problem solving. A sort of benevolent version of Borges's infinite library, where everything existed but, in this case, could also be retrieved and put to practical and imaginative use.

"The rise of the web was a rare instance when we learned new, positive information about human potential," Jaron Lanier wrote in his book *You Are Not a Gadget*. "Who would have guessed (at least at first) that millions of people would put so much effort into a project without the presence of advertising, commercial motive, threat of punishment, charismatic figures, identity politics, exploitation of the fear of death, or any of the other classic motivators of mankind. In vast numbers, people did something cooperatively, solely because it was a good idea, and it was beautiful."

At the heart of the collective enterprise in those early days, Lanier recalled, was "a sweet faith in human nature. If we empowered individuals, we believed, more good than harm would result. The way the internet has gone sour since then is truly perverse."

The same web that's democratized information, forced (some) governments to be more transparent, and enabled everyone from political dissidents to scientists and doctors to connect with one another— that same web, people are learning, can be exploited by bad actors to spread misinformation and disinformation, cruelty and prejudice. The possibility of anonymity on the web has promoted a toxic lack of accountability and enabled harassers and trolls. Giant Silicon Valley companies have collected user data on a scale rivaling that of the NSA. And the explosion of internet use has also amplified many of the dynamics already at play in contemporary culture: from the self-absorption of the "Me" and "selfie" generations, to the isolation of people in ideological silos and the relativization of truth.

The sheer volume of data on the web allows people to cherry-pick facts or factoids or nonfacts that support their own point of view, encouraging academics and amateurs alike to find material to support their theories rather than examining empirical evidence to come to rational conclusions. As Nicholas Carr, the former executive editor of the *Harvard Business Review*, wrote in *The Shallows: What the Internet Is Doing to Our Brains*, "We don't see the forest when we search the Web. We don't even see the trees. We see twigs and leaves."

On the web, where clicks are everything, and entertainment and news are increasingly blurred, material that is sensational, bizarre, or outrageous rises to the top, along with posts that cynically appeal to the reptilian part of our brains—to primitive emotions like fear and hate and anger.

In this era of nervous distraction and information overload, attention is the most precious commodity on the internet. And as the law professor Tim Wu observed in his book *The Attention Merchants*, sites gradually learned in the early 2010s how to make content consistently go viral: often the "urge to share was activated by a spectrum of 'high-arousal' emotions, like awe, outrage, and anxiety."

By 2015, Wu wrote, the web—once "a commons that fostered the amateur eccentric in every area of interest"—was overrun by "commercial junk, much of it directed at the very basest human impulses of voyeurism and titillation." There were "vast areas of darkness" now—like "the lands of the cajoling listicles and the celebrity nonstories"—that were "engineered for no purpose but to keep a public mindlessly clicking and sharing away, spreading the accompanying ads like a bad cold."

WHILE PUBLIC TRUST in the media declined in the new millennium (part of a growing mistrust of institutions and gatekeepers, as well as a concerted effort by the right wing to discredit the mainstream press), more and more people started getting their news through Facebook, Twitter, and other online sources: by 2017, two-thirds of Americans said they got at least some of their news through social media. This reliance on family and friends and Facebook and Twitter for news, however, would feed the ravenous monster of fake news.

Fake news is nothing new, of course: sensationalized press coverage helped drum up public support for the Spanish-American War, and Julius Caesar spun his conquest of Gaul as a preventive action. But the internet and social media allow rumors, speculation, and lies to flash around the world in a matter of seconds: like the preposterous Pizzagate stories and the baseless stories claiming that the man behind the massacre of fifty-eight people in Las Vegas in October 2017 was an anti-Trump liberal who followed MoveOn.org and had recently become a Muslim.

During the last three months of the 2016 presidential campaign, *BuzzFeed News* reported, "top-performing" fake election news stories on Facebook generated more reader engagement than top stories from major news organizations like *The New York Times, The Washington Post,* NBC News, and *The Huffington Post.* Of the twenty fake stories, all but three were pro-Trump or anti–Hillary Clinton, including one which claimed that Clinton had sold weapons to ISIS and another which claimed that the pope had endorsed Trump. A study from Oxford University's Internet Institute found that, on Twitter, a network of Trump supporters circulated more junk news than any other political group in the sample. And a 2018 *Politico* analysis found that voters in so-called news deserts—places with low numbers of news subscribers—went for Trump in greater numbers than voters in places where independent media could check his assertions.

As the role that social media had played in spreading fake news and enabling Russian efforts to interfere in the 2016 U.S. election became increasingly clear, some Silicon Valley insiders experienced a kind of existential crisis. They worried that the magical tools they had helped create were becoming Frankensteinian monsters. Pierre Omidyar, founder of eBay, wrote that "the monetization and manipulation of information is swiftly tearing us apart," and commissioned a white paper on the effect that social media was having on accountability and trust and our democracy.

"The system is failing," Tim Berners-Lee declared. He was still an optimist, he said, "but an optimist standing at the top of the hill with a nasty storm blowing in my face, hanging on to a fence."

In an impassioned essay, Roger McNamee, an early investor in Facebook, argued that the Russians' manipulation of Facebook, Twitter, Google, and other platforms to try to shift the outcomes of the 2016 U.S. election and the Brexit referendum was just the tip of a huge iceberg: unless fundamental changes were made, he warned, those platforms were going to be manipulated again, and "the level of political discourse, already in the gutter, was going to get even worse."

The problems were inherent, McNamee argued, in the algorithms used by platforms like Facebook to maximize user engagement. The more time members spend on a platform, the more ads a company sells and the more profits it makes, and the way to maximize engagement is by "sucking up and analyzing your data, using it to predict what will cause you to react most strongly, and then giving you more of that." This not only creates the filter bubbles that seal people off in partisan silos but also favors simplistic, provocative messages. Conspiracy theories easily go viral on social media. And so do dumbed-down, inflammatory political messages—like those retailed by the Trump campaign and the Vote Leave party in Britain, appealing to raw emotions like the fear of immigrants or anger over disappearing jobs. Such populist messages, historians attest, tend to gain traction during times of economic uncertainty (as in the lingering aftermath of the financial crisis of 2008 and snowballing income inequality) and cultural and social change (as with globalization and seismic technological innovation).

Trump's hate-fueled message was almost tailor-made for social media algorithms. Steve Bannon told the journalist Michael Lewis that Trump not only was an angry man but also had a unique ability to tap into the anger of others: "We got elected on Drain the Swamp, Lock Her Up, Build a Wall. This was pure anger. Anger and fear is what gets people to the polls."

At the same time, the Trump campaign made shrewd and Machiavellian use of social media and big-data tools, employing information from Facebook and Cambridge Analytica (a data science firm partially owned by the Trump backer and Breitbart investor Robert Mercer that boasts of its ability to psychologically profile millions of potential voters) to target its advertising and plan Trump's campaign stops.

Facebook revealed that the data of as many as 87 million people may have been shared improperly with Cambridge Analytica, which used the information to help create tools designed to predict and influence voter behavior. A former employee of Cambridge Analytica said that Steve Bannon oversaw a 2014 voter persuasion effort in which anti-establishment messages—like "drain the swamp" and "deep state"—were identified and tested.

The Trump campaign's digital director, Brad Parscale, recounted how they used Facebook's advertising tools to micro-target potential supporters with customized ads, making some fifty to sixty thousand ads a day, continually tweaking language, graphics, even colors, to try to elicit a favorable response.

The campaign also used so-called dark posts (visible only to the recipient) and launched three voter-suppression operations, according to a senior campaign official quoted in *Bloomberg Businessweek*: one was targeted at Bernie Sanders supporters; one at young women (who, the campaign thought, might be offended by reminders of Bill Clinton's philandering—odd, given Trump's own scandals with women); and one at African Americans (who the campaign thought might not vote for Clinton if reminded of her use of the term "super predators" in 1996, referring to her husband's anticrime initiative).

———

THE MASTER MANIPULATORS of social media in the 2016 election, of course, were the Russians whose long-term goal—to erode voters' faith in democracy and the electoral system—dovetailed with their short-term goal of tipping the outcome toward Trump. U.S. intelligence agencies also concluded that Russian hackers stole emails from the Democratic National Committee, which were later provided to WikiLeaks. These plots were all part of a concerted effort by the Kremlin, stepped up since Putin's reelection in 2012, to use asymmetrical, nonmilitary means to achieve its goals of weakening the European Union and NATO and undermining faith in globalism and Western democratic liberalism. Toward such ends, Russia has been supporting populist parties in Europe, like Marine Le Pen's far-right National Front party in France, and has interfered in the elections of at least nineteen European countries in recent years. It also continues to wage disinformation campaigns through state media outlets like Sputnik and RT.

In the case of the American election, Facebook told Congress that Russian operatives published some eighty thousand posts on Facebook between June 2015 and August 2017 that might have been seen by 126 million Americans; that's more than half the number of people registered to vote in the country. Some of the Russian posts actively tried to promote Trump or damage Clinton; others were simply meant to widen existing divisions in American society over issues like race, immigration, and gun rights. For instance, there was a post from a phony group named South United, showing a Confederate flag and "a call for the South to rise again." Another from a phony group called Blacktivist, memorializing the Black Panthers. And a Facebook ad called "Secured Borders," showing a sign saying, "No Invaders Allowed."

"The strategy is to take a crack in our society and turn it into a chasm," said Senator Angus King of Maine during a Senate Intelligence Committee hearing on Russian interference in the election.

Reporting from several publications found that YouTube's recommendation engine seemed to be steering viewers toward divisive, sensationalistic, and conspiracy-minded content. And Twitter found that more than fifty thousand Russia-linked accounts on its platform were posting material about the 2016 election. A report from Oxford University found that in the run-up to the election the number of links on Twitter to "Russian news stories, unverified or irrelevant links to WikiLeaks pages, or junk news" exceeded the number of links to professionally researched and published news. The report also found that "average levels of misinformation were higher in swing states"—like Florida, North Carolina, and Virginia—than in uncontested states.

Russians had become very adept not only at generating fake news but also at inventing fake Americans who commented on that fake news and joined fake American groups. A Russian troll factory employee named Vitaly Bespalov, who worked at a St. Petersburg propaganda factory called the Internet Research Agency, told NBC News that the job was "a merry-go-round of lies." Workers on the first floor wrote fake news stories referencing blog posts written by workers on the third floor, while colleagues posted comments on those stories under fake names and coordinated other social media posts. According to U.S. intelligence sources, some of the IRA's accounts had been producing pro-Russian propaganda about Ukraine but switched over to pro-Trump messages as early as December 2015.

When the *Access Hollywood* tape of Trump talking about groping women came out before the election, Russian Twitter agents rushed to his rescue, trashing the mainstream media and trying to refocus attention on damaging emails hacked from Clinton's campaign chairman, John Podesta. This sort of support for Trump continued after he took up residence in the

White House, with pro-Kremlin Twitter accounts trying to stir up trouble over matters like the controversy of NFL players taking a knee. By the end of 2017, however, these Russian accounts seemed to be increasingly focused on undermining special counsel Robert Mueller and his investigation into Russian interference in the election.

Russia also appears to have jumped into the U.S. debate over the Trump administration's determination to repeal net neutrality—a move that was opposed by 83 percent of Americans in a poll taken shortly before the FCC voted to do away with the Obama-era rules that required internet providers to treat all web traffic equally. Before announcing its decision, the FCC had said it welcomed public comment on the issue, but it appears that many of the comments it received were fakes or duplicates. One study found that 444,938 comments came from Russian email addresses and that more than 7.75 million comments came from email domains associated with FakeMailGenerator .com and contained virtually identical wording.

Troll factories and bot armies are used by political parties and governments of countries like Russia, Turkey, and Iran to spread propaganda, harass dissenters, flood social networks with misinformation, and create the illusion of popularity or momentum through likes, retweets, or shares. An Oxford University study noted, "Sometimes, when political parties or candidates use social media manipulation as part of their campaign strategy, these tactics are continued when they assume power. For example, in the Philippines, many of the so-called 'keyboard trolls' hired to spread propaganda for presidential candidate Duterte during the election continue to spread and amplify messages in support of his policies now that he's in power."

THE USE OF bots in manipulating public opinion is just one of the factors examined in the Omidyar Group report on social media's effect on public discourse. In addition to amplifying polarization, the report concluded, social media tends to undermine trust in institutions and makes it more difficult to have the sorts of fact-based debates and discussions that are essential to democracy. The micro-targeted ads on social media and the algorithms designed to customize people's news feeds blur the distinctions between what is popular and what is verifiable, and diminish the ability of people to take part in a shared conversation.

Things are only likely to get worse, particularly

if the Trump White House remains in denial about Russian interference in the election and fails to take action against what Michael Hayden, a former director of the NSA and the CIA, has called the "most successful covert-influence operation in history." The head of the Cyber Division at the Department of Homeland Security revealed that the Russians attempted to break into the election systems in twenty-one states during the 2016 election and successfully penetrated a few. And a computer security firm reported that the same Russian hackers who stole DNC emails in 2016 were targeting Senate accounts in the run-up to the 2018 midterms.

Russia already tried to meddle in elections in Germany, France, and the Netherlands, as well as the Brexit referendum in the U.K., and the ease with which it interfered in the 2016 U.S. election (and the lack of penalties it suffered in year one of the Trump administration) have surely emboldened it. Politicians in Mexico and other countries now fear they might be next on Putin's hit list and are bracing for destabilizing waves of fake news and propaganda.

Technological developments are likely to complicate matters further. Advances in virtual reality and machine-learning systems will soon result in fabricated images and videos so convincing that they may be difficult to distinguish from the real thing. Voices can already be re-created from audio samples, and facial expressions can be manipulated by AI programs. In the future, we could be exposed to realistic videos of politicians saying things they never said: Baudrillard's simulacrum come to life. These are *Black Mirror*–like developments that will complicate our ability to distinguish between the imitation and the real, the fake and the true.

8

"THE FIREHOSE OF FALSEHOOD"

PROPAGANDA AND FAKE NEWS

You can sway a thousand men by appealing to their prejudices quicker than you can convince one man by logic.

—Robert A. Heinlein

Russia is at the center of political conversations in America and Europe because of Russian interference in the 2016 U.S. presidential election and a host of other elections around the world. The methods used by Russia in these operations are reminders of the sophisticated propaganda machine that the Kremlin has built over the decades, going back to the Cold War, and its new mastery of cyber warfare, including hacking, fake news, and the weaponized use of social media. At the same time, not so coincidentally, the thinking of two Russian figures—Vladimir Lenin and the much lesser known Vladislav Surkov, a former postmodernist theater director who's been described as "Putin's Rasputin" and the Kremlin's propaganda puppet master—informs many of the troubling political and social dynamics at work in the post-truth era.

Almost a century after his death, Lenin's model of revolution has proven frighteningly durable. His goal—not to improve the state machine, but to smash it and all its institutions—has been embraced by many twenty-first-century populists. And so have many of his tactics, from his use of confusion and chaos as tools to rally the masses, to his simplistic (and always broken) utopian promises, to his violent rhetoric attacking anything that could possibly be tarred as part of the status quo.

His incendiary language, Lenin once explained, was "calculated to evoke hatred, aversion and contempt"; such wording was "calculated not to convince, but to break up the ranks of the opponent, not to correct the mistake of the opponent, but to destroy him, to wipe his organization off the face of the earth. This wording is indeed of such a nature as to evoke the worst thoughts, the worst suspicions about the opponent." All of which sounds a lot like a template for the sort of language employed by Trump and his supporters in attacking Hillary Clinton during the 2016 campaign ("Lock her up!"), the sort of language employed by radical supporters of the Vote Leave campaign in Britain, the sort of language increasingly employed by right-wing populist movements on both sides of the Atlantic.

The journalist Anne Applebaum identified an entire group of "neo-Bolsheviks"—including Trump, Nigel Farage in Britain, Marine Le Pen in France, Jarosław Kaczyński in Poland, and the Hungarian prime minister Viktor Orbán—who, like Lenin and Trotsky, started out on the political fringes and rode a wave of populism to prominent positions. In 2017, she wrote that "to an extraordinary degree, they have adopted Lenin's refusal to compromise, his anti-democratic elevation of some social groups over others and his hateful attacks on his 'illegitimate' opponents."

Many of the more successful neo-Bolsheviks, Applebaum points out, have created their own "alternative media" that specializes in disinformation, hatemongering, and the trolling of adversaries. Lying is both reflexive and a matter of conviction: they believe, she writes, "that ordinary morality does not apply to them. . . . In a rotten world, truth can be sacrificed in the name of 'the People,' or as a means of targeting 'Enemies of the People.' In the struggle for power, anything is permitted."

In fact, the historian Victor Sebestyen writes in a biography of Lenin that the Bolshevik leader was "the godfather of what commentators a century after his time call 'post-truth politics,'" and he stands, in many respects, as a "thoroughly modern political phenomenon—the kind of demagogue familiar to us in Western democracies, as well as in dictatorships." Anyone, Sebestyen adds, "who has lived through recent elections in the supposedly sophisticated political cultures of the West might recognize him."

Steve Bannon, Trump's now estranged adviser and the former executive chairman of Breitbart News, once described himself to a journalist as "a Leninist." Writing in *The Daily Beast* in 2013, Ronald Radosh recounted that Bannon declared, "Lenin wanted to destroy the state, and that's my goal, too. I want to bring everything crashing down, and destroy all of today's establishment." The conservative billionaire Robert Mercer, who helped finance Cambridge Analytica, thinks the less government the better. A former high-level employee of Mercer's hedge fund told *The New Yorker*'s Jane Mayer: "He wants it to all fall down."

NOT SURPRISINGLY, the two countries to master the black arts of propaganda in the twentieth century were the totalitarian states of Nazi Germany and the Soviet Union. Their techniques of manipulating the public and promoting their hateful ideologies have trickled down to several generations of autocrats and demagogues around the world. Lenin specialized in promises he would never keep. "He offered simple solutions to complex problems," Sebestyen wrote in his biography of the Bolshevik leader. "He lied unashamedly. He identified a scapegoat he could later label 'enemies of the people.' He justified himself on the basis that winning meant everything: the ends justified the means."

Hitler devoted whole chapters of *Mein Kampf* to the subject of propaganda, and his pronouncements, along with those of his propaganda minister, Joseph Goebbels, would constitute a kind of playbook for aspiring autocrats: appeal to people's emotions, not their intellects; use "stereotyped formulas," repeated over and over again; continuously assail opponents and label them with distinctive phrases or slogans that will elicit visceral reactions from the audience.

Described by biographers as a narcissist with a taste for self-dramatization, Hitler possessed an instinctive sense of how to capture public attention from the start. "Who cares whether they laugh at us or insult us, treating us as fools or criminals?" he wrote about his early efforts to make a name for himself. "The point is that they talk about us and constantly think about us." Like Lenin, he also underscored the need "to disrupt the existing order of things" and "thus make room for the penetration" of new doctrines.

In *The Origins of Totalitarianism*, Hannah Arendt looked at the essential role that propaganda played in gaslighting the populations of Nazi Germany and Soviet Russia, writing that "in an ever-changing, incomprehensible world the masses had reached the point where they would, at the same time, believe everything and nothing, think that everything was possible and that nothing was true."

"Mass propaganda," she wrote, "discovered that its audience was ready at all times to believe the worst, no matter how absurd, and did not particularly object to being deceived because it held every statement to be a lie anyhow. The totalitarian mass leaders based their propaganda on the correct psychological assumption that, under such conditions, one could make people believe the most fantastic statements one day, and trust that if the next day they were given irrefutable proof of their falsehood, they would take refuge in cynicism; instead of deserting the leaders who had lied to them, they would protest that they had known all along that the statement was a lie and would admire the leaders for their superior tactical cleverness."

Russia still uses propaganda to achieve these very same ends: to distract and exhaust its own people (and increasingly, citizens of foreign countries), to wear them down through such a profusion of lies that they cease to resist and retreat back into their private lives. A Rand Corporation report called this Putin model of propaganda "the firehose of falsehood"—an unremitting, high-intensity stream of lies, partial truths, and complete fictions spewed forth with tireless aggression to obfuscate the truth and overwhelm and confuse anyone trying to pay attention.

"Russian propaganda makes no commitment to objective reality," the report observes: manufactured sources are sometimes used, and so is manufactured evidence (faked photographs, faked on-scene news reporting, staged footage with actors playing victims of manufactured atrocities or crimes). "Russian news channels, such as RT and Sputnik News," the report goes on, "are more like a blend of infotainment and disinformation than fact-checked journalism, though their formats intentionally take the appearance of proper news programs."

Russian propaganda, which was extensively exported in the run-up to the 2016 U.S. election and elections in Europe, is cranked out quickly in response to breaking news, and it's endlessly recycled, in high volume at high spin rates, through various media channels to feed the perception of multiple sources. Because Russian trolls are unconcerned with veracity or inconsistencies, they can often get their fictional version of events out before legitimate news organizations can post accurate accounts, taking advantage of the psychological tendency of people to accept the first information received on a topic (and, as the Rand report observes, then "favor this information when faced with conflicting messages").

The sheer volume of *dezinformatsiya* unleashed by the Russian firehose system—much like the more improvised but equally voluminous stream of lies, scandals, and shocks emitted by Trump, his GOP enablers, and media apparatchiks—tends to overwhelm and numb people while simultaneously defining deviancy down and normalizing the unacceptable. Outrage gives way to outrage fatigue, which gives way to the sort of cynicism and weariness that empowers those disseminating the lies. As the former world chess champion and Russian pro-democracy leader Garry Kasparov tweeted in December 2016, "The point of modern propaganda isn't only to misinform or push an agenda. It is to exhaust your critical thinking, to annihilate truth."

Choose your metaphor: muddying the waters, throwing chum to the sharks, cranking up the fog machine, flinging gorilla dust in the public's eyes: it's a tactic designed to create adrenal fatigue and news exhaustion, a strategy perfectly designed for our ADD, information-overloaded age, "this twittering world," in T. S. Eliot's words, where people can be "distracted from distraction by distraction."

In the digital era, sowing confusion online through a barrage of misinformation and disinformation is actually becoming the go-to tactic of propagandists around the world, says the scholar Zeynep Tufekci in her insightful book *Twitter and Tear Gas*.

"In the networked public sphere," Tufekci writes, "the goal of the powerful often is not to convince people of the truth of a particular narrative or to block a particular piece of information from getting out (that is increasingly difficult), but to produce resignation, cynicism, and a sense of disempowerment among the people." This can be done, she notes, in a variety of

ways: inundating audiences with information; producing distractions to dilute their attention and focus;
delegitimizing media that provides accurate information; deliberately sowing confusion, fear, and doubt;
creating or claiming hoaxes; and "generating harass-
ment campaigns designed to make it harder for cred-
ible conduits of information to operate."

THE CONTEMPORARY Russian master of propaganda
Vladislav Surkov, who's been called "the real genius
of the Putin era," has employed all these techniques
and more in helping to engineer Putin's rise to—and
consolidation of—power. In fact, the tradecraft of the
Russian agents who carried out a sophisticated campaign of disinformation during the 2016 presidential
campaign bears many of the hallmarks of Surkov's
stage management.

The journalist Peter Pomerantsev, the author of
the book *Nothing Is True and Everything Is Possible*,
has described Surkov as the impresario who turned
Russian politics into a reality show in which "democratic institutions are maintained without any democratic freedoms."

"He helped invent a new strain of authoritarian-
ism based not on crushing opposition from above,"

Pomerantsev wrote in 2014, "but on climbing into different interest groups and manipulating them from inside." For instance: "Nationalist leaders like Vladimir Zhirinovsky would play the right-wing buffoon to make Mr. Putin look moderate by contrast."

"With one hand," Pomerantsev went on, "Mr. Surkov supported human rights groups made up of former dissidents; with the other he organized pro-Kremlin youth groups like Nashi, which accused human rights leaders of being tools of the West." Playing all sides against one another to create chaos was a way to ensure that the Kremlin held all the puppets' strings while using disinformation to remake reality.

This same sort of Surkovian manipulation informed Russian efforts to disrupt the 2016 U.S. election by impersonating Americans and grassroots political groups on social media. As described in a thirty-seven-page indictment brought by the special counsel Robert Mueller, the scheme was a sophisticated one involving hundreds of operatives working for the Internet Research Agency (the Russian troll farm based in St. Petersburg). These agents—some of whom visited the United States under false pretenses—set up hundreds of fake social media accounts, posing as (and sometimes stealing the identities of) real Americans and using an American server to mask their location in Russia. Using these fictional personas, the Russians posted material on Facebook, Instagram, Twitter, and YouTube and built up substantial followings. Their mission: to spread derogatory information about Hillary Clinton (and during the primaries Ted Cruz and Marco Rubio) and distrust about the political system in general. In addition to trying to widen schisms among voters over issues like immigration, religion, and race, the Russians spread fake news aimed at boosting Trump's popularity and hurting Clinton's. They also helped organize and promote pro-Trump rallies, spread rumors of voter fraud by the Democratic Party, and began "to encourage U.S. minority groups not to vote" in the election, or to vote for a third-party candidate.

Some of the Russian operatives' moves seemed like cynical pieces of Surkovian stagecraft: recruiting a real American to hold a sign depicting Clinton and a phony quotation attributed to her, "I think Sharia Law will be a powerful new direction of freedom"; hiring one American to build a large cage on a flatbed truck and a second American to wear a costume portraying Clinton in a prison uniform.

SURKOV'S GOAL IN Russia was always the same, Pomerantsev argued in *Politico*: "to keep the great, 140-million-strong population reeling with oohs and aahs about gays and God, Satan, fascists, the CIA, and far-fetched geopolitical nightmares." Ensuring that the country was always off balance and a little paranoid was a way to keep people preoccupied while encouraging them "to look to the 'strong hand' of the Kremlin for protection."

In addition to his background in both theater and public relations, Surkov was also a self-styled bohemian who liked to allude to avant-garde artists and postmodernist thinkers. He helped turn Russian television, in Pomerantsev's words, into "a kitsch Putin-worshipping propaganda machine"—not dull and ham-handed like old Soviet TV, but superficially glitzy in a way that weaponized Western entertainment for Russian ends.

Surkov's orchestration of Kremlin propaganda has been described as having a performance-art quality to it—stage-managed spectacle meant less to convey an old-school Soviet message than to create multiple, often conflicting story lines that promote confusion and blur reality and fiction. There is no Communist ideology in Putin and Surkov's Russia, just what

Pomerantsev called "power for power's sake and the accumulation of vast wealth."

In the service of this nihilistic vision, Surkov has invoked arguments repudiating the existence of objective truth. He has written that "hypocrisy in the rationalistic paradigm of Western civilization is inevitable" because "speech is too linear, too formal to fully reflect the so-called reality," and because "pretending to be what you are not, to hide your intentions is the most important technology of biological survival." In Homer's classics, he notes, the earnest Achilles is less compelling than the "cunning" Odysseus—a kind of trickster hero, adept at lies and deceit—who is the one who survives. All narratives are contingent, Surkov suggests, and all politicians are liars; therefore, the alternative facts put out by the Kremlin (and by Donald Trump) are just as valid as anyone else's.

In November 2017, the Russian site RT published an essay by Surkov that invoked Derrida-inspired arguments about the unreliability of language—and the gap between words and meaning—to suggest that Western notions of truthfulness and transparency are naive and unsophisticated. At once arch and convoluted, the piece embodied Surkov's transactional view of the world, privileging irony over sincerity, trickery over earnestness, while name-dropping pop allusions—like the heavy metal band Five Finger Death Punch (Surkov approvingly quoted the lyrics to "Wash It All Away").

Surkov's essay ends with a portentous account about how the Roman Empire replaced the Roman Republic, suggesting that the republic failed because it became entangled in its "sophisticated system of checks and balances" and needed "the help of a simple imperial vertical." He ominously suggests that America, too, is waiting to be pulled from growing chaos by "a strong hand." An argument that echoes the thinking of a right-wing, antidemocratic philosophy known as "neoreaction" or "NRx," which is gathering followers in the United States and envisions the elevation of a leader who would run the country as a kind of unshackled CEO.

"The king of the West," Surkov wrote in his RT essay, "the founder of the digital dictatorship, the leader with semi-artificial intelligence has already been predicted by comic books. Why do not these comic books come true?"

9

THE
SCHADENFREUDE
OF THE TROLLS

Introduce a little anarchy. Upset the established order, and everything becomes chaos. I'm an agent of chaos.

—THE JOKER IN *THE DARK KNIGHT*

WHILE SURKOV SEEMS INTENT ON EX-porting Russian nihilism to the West, along with antidemocratic principles and a disdain for truth, America has been grappling with a growing cynicism of its own. And fueled by mistrust and some goading from the Far Right, that cynicism was beginning to calcify, in the opening decades of the twenty-first century, into a kind of homegrown nihilism. It was partly a by-product of disillusion with a grossly dysfunctional political system that runs on partisan warfare; partly a sense of dislocation in a world reeling from technological change, globalization, and data overload; and partly a reflection of dwindling hopes among the middle class that the basic promises of the American dream—an affordable house, a decent education, and a brighter future for their kids—were achievable in a post-2008-crash United States. While the too-big-to-fail banks paid little price for the crash of 2008, many working people were still trying to make up lost ground. Income inequality was rising, the cost of a college education had exploded, and affordable housing was slipping out of reach.

It's a mind-set that made a lot of voters susceptible to Trump's attacks on the status quo and that made some try to churlishly rationalize his transactional politics and shamelessness: Why get upset by his lies, when all politicians lie? Why get upset by his venality, when the law of the jungle rules? In this respect, Donald Trump is as much a symptom of the times as he is a dangerous catalyst. That he broke most of his promises with astonishing alacrity only served to increase many people's cynicism: a mood that is not conducive to civic engagement and that, ironically, fuels Trump's attacks on our ideals and our institutions.

As his own books make clear, Trump is completely lacking in empathy and has always had a dog-eat-dog view of the world: kill or be killed, and always get even. It's a relentlessly dark view, shaped by his domineering father, Fred, who gave him a zero-sum perspective, and by his early mentor Roy Cohn, who gave him the advice, when in trouble, "Attack, attack, attack."

"The world is a horrible place," Trump declared in his book *Think Big*. "Lions kill for food, but people kill for sport." And: "The same burning greed that makes people loot, kill, and steal in emergencies like fires and floods, operates daily in normal everyday people. It lurks right beneath the surface, and when you least expect it, it rears its nasty head and bites you. Accept it. The world is a brutal place. People will annihilate you just for the fun of it or to show off to their friends."

Trump defines himself largely through the people and institutions he attacks (Hillary Clinton, Barack Obama, James Comey, the press, the intelligence agencies, the FBI, the judiciary, anyone he perceives as a rival or a threat), and he always seems on the look-out for an enemy or a scapegoat, insulting immigrants, Muslims, women, and African Americans. Much of his agenda, for that matter, is driven by negativity— by an urge to undo President Obama's legacy, including health care and environmental protection, and also to dismantle the broader safety net and civil liberties protections implemented since Lyndon B.

Johnson launched the Great Society back in the mid-1960s. "Make America Great Again" translates into turning the clock back to the 1950s, before the civil rights movement, before the women's movement, before LGBT rights, before Black Lives Matter.

But Trump is hardly alone in his negativity and nihilism. Many Republicans in Congress have also abandoned reason, common sense, and the deliberative process of policy making. Some freely acknowledged that they voted for the tax bill because of their big-money donors. Representative Chris Collins said, "My donors are basically saying, 'Get it done or don't ever call me again.'" Congress has failed to act on immigration reform again and again, and it's refused to act on gun control year after year, tragedy after tragedy.

When it comes to dealing with President Trump, many of these same Republicans simply ignore his multiplying lies; his appointment of woefully unqualified nominees to important government posts; his haphazard and cavalier scuttling of decades of domestic and foreign policy; his reckless decision making (which often seems to emerge, to use Pynchon's words in *Gravity's Rainbow*, from "a chaos of peeves, whims, hallucinations and all-round assholery"). They might confide their worries about Trump's competence or stability to reporters—off the record, of course—but they won't say so in public for fear of jeopardizing their standing with Trump's base. This sort of cynical partisanship only serves to turn voters' disgust with the government into a self-fulfilling prophecy.

THE NIHILISM IN Washington is both an echo and a cause of more widespread feelings: a reflection of a growing loss of faith in institutions and a loss of respect for both the rule of law and everyday norms and traditions; a symptom of our loss of civility, our growing inability to have respectful debates with people who have opinions different from our own; and our growing unwillingness to give others the benefit of the doubt, room for an honest mistake, the courtesy of a hearing.

It's a sense that life is random and devoid of meaning, combined with a carelessness about consequences. Think of the Buchanans in *The Great Gatsby*: "They were careless people, Tom and Daisy—they smashed up things and creatures and then retreated back into their money or their vast carelessness, or whatever it was that kept them together, and let other people clean up the mess they had made." And it's reflected in the cult popularity of *Fight Club* and Michel Houellebecq's willfully repellent novels and the mainstream appreciation of bleakly brilliant works like Cormac McCarthy's *No Country for Old Men* and Nic Pizzolatto's HBO series *True Detective*.

The new nihilism is WikiLeaks failing to scrub the names of Afghan civilians who might have had contact with American troops from classified U.S. documents it released—a move that human rights groups like Amnesty International warned could have "deadly ramifications" for the people named.

The new nihilism is people making money by creating fake news stories—by one estimate upward of ten thousand dollars a month, earned through online ads. NPR reported that one entirely fictional story with this headline—"FBI Agent Suspected in Hillary Email Leaks Found Dead in Apparent Murder-Suicide"—was shared on Facebook more than half a million times and was created by a California-based company named Disinfomedia that oversees several fake news sites. The founder of Disinfomedia, identified by NPR as one Jestin Coler, claimed that he started the company to show how easily fake news spreads and that he enjoys "the game." He said that he and his writers "tried to do similar things to liberals" but those efforts didn't go viral the way stories aimed at Trump supporters do.

The new nihilism is Michael Anton—who became a senior national security official in the Trump administration—writing an article (under the pseudonym Publius Decius Mus) titled "The Flight 93 Election," in which he compared the plight of voters in 2016 to that of the passengers on the doomed airplane that went down on 9/11 and compared voting for Trump to charging the cockpit. "Charge the cockpit or you die," he wrote. "You may die anyway. You—or the leader of your party—may make it into the cockpit and not know how to fly or land the plane. There are no guarantees. Except one: if you don't try, death is certain."

The new nihilism manifests itself in grotesque acts of cruelty like trolling the grieving parents of children murdered in Sandy Hook and accusing them of perpetrating a hoax, and similar attacks on the students who survived the Parkland school massacre. Given such events, it's not surprising that one of the most popular words in the Trump era is "weaponize"—as in weaponizing irony, weaponizing fear, weaponizing memes, weaponizing lies, weaponizing the tax code.

The most appalling racist, sexist, and perversely

cruel remarks are served up on social media, often with a wink or a sneer, and when called out, practitioners frequently respond that they were simply joking—much the way that White House aides say Trump is simply joking or misunderstood when he makes offensive remarks. At a November 2016 alt-right conference, the white supremacist Richard Spencer ended his speech, shouting, "Hail Trump! Hail our people! Hail victory!" When asked about the Nazi salutes that greeted his exclamation, Spencer replied that they were "clearly done in a spirit of irony and exuberance."

As the researchers Alice Marwick and Rebecca Lewis suggest in their *Media Manipulation and Disinformation Online* study, ironic fascism can become a kind of gateway drug, leading to the unironic version: "A 4chan troll may be more receptive to serious white supremacist claims after using ethnic slurs 'ironically' for two or three months."

In fact, *The Huffington Post* reported that the neo-Nazi site *The Daily Stormer* (which aims "to spread the message of nationalism and anti-Semitism to the masses") has a style guide for writers. It provides suggestions like "Always blame the Jews for everything," approved lists of racial slurs, and this chilling tip on using humor: "The tone of the site should be light."

"The unindoctrinated should not be able to tell if we are joking or not," the author of the style guide advised. "There should also be a conscious awareness of mocking stereotypes of hateful racists. I usually think of this as self-deprecating humor—I am a racist making fun of stereotypes of racists, because I don't take myself super-seriously.

"This is obviously a ploy and I actually do want to gas kikes. But that's neither here nor there."

TRUMP, OF COURSE, is a troll—both by temperament and by habit. His tweets and offhand taunts are the very essence of trolling—the lies, the scorn, the invective, the trash talk, and the rabid non sequiturs of an angry, aggrieved, isolated, and deeply self-absorbed adolescent who lives in a self-constructed bubble and gets the attention he craves from bashing his enemies and trailing clouds of outrage and dismay in his path. Even as president, he continues to troll individuals and institutions, tweeting and retweeting insults, fake news, and treacherous innuendo. On Christmas Eve of 2017, he retweeted an image showing a splotch of blood, labeled CNN, on the sole of his shoe, once again denigrating the press. When another Twitter user called him "the

159

most superior troll on the whole of twitter" in 2013, Trump replied, "A great compliment!"

In his revealing 2017 book, *Devil's Bargain*, the journalist Joshua Green reported that in the wake of Gamergate, Steve Bannon recruited a lot of gamers— young, alienated, mostly white men—to Breitbart. Although many were not particularly ideologically in- clined to begin with, they were eager to throw bombs at the establishment and saw Trump as a kind of kin- dred soul. "Trump himself," Green writes, "would help cement this alt-right alliance by retweeting images of Pepe the Frog and occasional missives—always inad- vertently, his staff insisted—from white nationalist Twitter accounts."

Some trolls have employed relativistic arguments to insist that their promotion of alternative facts is simply adding a voice to the conversation, that there are no more objective truths anymore—only different perceptions and different story lines. They are clearly using postmodernist arguments in bad faith, but their assertions are no more disingenuous, really, than the efforts of Paul de Man's defenders to explain away his anti-Semitism by using deconstruction to argue that the articles he wrote for a pro-Nazi publication in the 1940s didn't really mean what they appear to mean.

Deconstruction, in fact, is deeply nihilistic, implying that the efforts of journalists and historians—to ascertain the best available truths through the careful gathering and weighing of evidence—are futile. It suggests that reason is an outdated value, that language is not a tool for communication but an unstable and deceptive interface that is constantly subverting itself. Proponents of deconstruction don't believe that the intent of an author confers meaning on a text (they think that's up to the reader/viewer/recipient), and many postmodernists go so far as to suggest that the idea of individual responsibility is overrated, as the scholar Christopher Butler puts it, for promoting "a far too novelistic and bourgeois belief in the importance of individual human agency in preference to an attribution to underlying economic structures."

In the 1960s, when postmodernism took off in Europe and the United States, it was an antiauthoritarian doctrine, proposing an overthrow of old humanistic traditions, and as its tenets of irony, self-consciousness, and sarcasm leaked into popular culture, it could be seen, as David Foster Wallace observed in the early 1990s, as an antidote to the hypocrisy and smugness of the 1950s world of *Leave It to Beaver;* it was a "bad-boy" means of exploding old pieties and conventions at a time when the world seemed increasingly absurd. It also led to some genuinely innovative and daring art like Wallace's own *Infinite Jest*.

In a long essay about contemporary culture, Wallace argued that while postmodern irony could be a potent instrument for blowing things up, it was essentially a "critical and destructive" theory—good at ground clearing, yet singularly "unuseful when it comes to constructing anything to replace the hypocrisies it debunks." Its promulgation of cynicism made writers wary of sincerity and "retrovalues like originality, depth, and integrity," he wrote; it shielded "the heaper of scorn from scorn" while congratulating "the patron of scorn for rising above the mass of people who still fall for outmoded pretensions." The attitude of "I don't really mean what I say" would be adopted by those alt-right trolls who wanted to pretend that they weren't really bigots—they were just joking.

Two of the celebrities Wallace held up in 1993 as symbols of the poisonousness of postmodernist irony can now be seen, in retrospect, as harbingers of Trump. The first was Joe Isuzu, the star of jokey 1980s Isuzu car commercials—"an oily, Satanic-looking salesman," in Wallace's words, who "told whoppers about Isuzus' genuine llama-skin upholstery and ability to run on tap water"—a parody of a dishonest salesman who invited viewers "to congratulate themselves for getting the joke." Joe Isuzu liked to say "You have my word on it!" while a silent disclaimer ran over the footage of his boasts: "He's lying." A second celebrity Wallace held up as a tower of 1990s postmodern irony was Rush Limbaugh, whom he described as embodying "a hatred that winks and nudges you and pretends it's just kidding."

The trickle-down legacy of postmodernism, Wallace argued, was "sarcasm, cynicism, a manic ennui, suspicion of all authority, suspicion of all constraints on conduct, and a terrible penchant for ironic diagnosis of unpleasantness instead of an ambition not just to diagnose and ridicule but to redeem. You've got to understand that this stuff has permeated the culture. It's become our language"—"Postmodern irony's become our environment." The water in which we swim.

EPILOGUE

I N HIS CLEAR-EYED 1985 BOOK, *AMUSING OUR-selves to Death*, Neil Postman argued that "the technological distractions made possible by the electric plug" were indelibly altering our cultural discourse, making it more trivial, more inconsequential, and rendering the information it conveyed "simplistic, nonsubstantive, nonhistorical, and noncontextual; that is to say, information packaged as entertainment."

"Our priests and presidents, our surgeons and lawyers, our educators and newscasters," Postman wrote, "need worry less about satisfying the demands of their discipline than the demands of good showmanship."

By "electric plug," Postman meant television, but his observations apply even more fittingly to the age of the internet, in which data overload ensures that it's the shiniest object—the loudest voice, the most outrageous opinion—that captures our attention and receives the most clicks and buzz.

In *Amusing Ourselves to Death*, Postman compared

the dystopian vision that Aldous Huxley mapped out in *Brave New World* (in which people lead soporific lives, deadened by drugs and frivolous entertainments) with the one Orwell created in *1984* (in which people live under the crushing autocratic rule of Big Brother).

"Orwell feared those who would deprive us of information," Postman wrote. "Huxley feared those who would give us so much that we would be reduced to passivity and egoism. Orwell feared that the truth would be concealed from us. Huxley feared the truth would be drowned in a sea of irrelevance."

As Postman saw it, Huxley's dystopia was already coming to fruition in the late twentieth century. While Orwell's fears of a totalitarian state applied to the Soviet Union, Postman argued, the threat to the liberal democracies of the West—this was in 1985, remember—was better represented by Huxley's nightmare of a population too narcotized by "undisguised trivialities" to engage as responsible citizens.

These observations of Postman's were ahead of their time, and they would be echoed by George Saunders, who in an essay titled "The Braindead Megaphone" (2007) argued that our national discourse had been dangerously degraded by years of coverage of O. J. Simpson and Monica Lewinsky. Our national language, he wrote, had become so dumbed down—at once "aggressive, anxiety-provoking, maudlin, polarizing"—that "we were sitting ducks" when it came time to try to have a serious debate about whether to invade Iraq, and all we had in our hands was "the set of crude, hyperbolic tools we'd been using to discuss O.J., et al.": the shouted babblings of a loud know-it-all, know-nothing figure he called Megaphone Guy, bellowing into a bullhorn, its intelligence level set to "Stupid," its volume stuck on "Drown Out All Others."

But prescient as Postman's observations about Huxley are (and as prescient as Huxley was about our new age of distraction), it's clear that he also underestimated the relevance of Orwell's dystopia. Or perhaps it's the case that Trump and the assaults he and his administration have committed against the very idea of truth have made *1984* timely again—something readers recognized, propelling it and Hannah Arendt's *The Origins of Totalitarianism* up the bestseller lists in the month that Trump took the oath of office.

Trump's lies, his efforts to redefine reality, his violation of norms and rules and traditions, his mainstreaming of hate speech, his attacks on the press, the judiciary, the electoral system—all are reasons that the democracy watchdog group Freedom House warned that year one of the Trump administration had brought "further, faster erosion of America's own democratic standards than at any other time in memory," and all are reasons that Orwell's portrait of an authoritarian state, in which Big Brother tries to control all narratives and define the present and the past, is newly relevant.

TRUMP OFTEN SEEMS like a one-man set of Aesop-like fables—with easy-to-decipher morals like "those who lie down with dogs will get up with fleas" or "when someone tells you who he is, believe him"— but because he is president of the United States, his actions do not simply end in a tagline moral; rather, they ripple outward like a toxic tsunami, creating havoc in the lives of millions. Once he has left office, the damage he has done to American institutions and the country's foreign policy will take years to repair. And to the degree that his election was a reflection of larger dynamics in society—from the growing partisanship in politics, to the profusion of fake stories on social media, to our isolation in filter bubbles— his departure from the scene will not restore truth to health and well-being, at least not right away.

Philip Roth said he could never have imagined that "the 21st-century catastrophe to befall the U.S.A., the most debasing of disasters," would appear in "the ominously ridiculous commedia dell'arte figure of the boastful buffoon." Trump's ridiculousness, his narcissistic ability to make everything about himself, the outrageousness of his lies, and the profundity of his ignorance can easily distract attention from the more lasting implications of his story: how easily Republicans in Congress enabled him, undermining the whole concept of checks and balances set in place by the founders; how a third of the country passively accepted his assaults on the Constitution; how easily Russian disinformation took root in a culture where the teaching of history and civics had seriously atrophied.

GEORGE WASHINGTON's Farewell Address of 1796 was eerily clairvoyant about the dangers America now faces. In order to protect its future, he said, the young country must guard its Constitution and remain vigilant about efforts to sabotage the separation and balance of powers within the government that he and the other founders had so carefully crafted.

Washington warned about the rise of "cunning, ambitious, and unprincipled men" who might try "to subvert the power of the people" and "usurp for themselves the reins of government, destroying afterwards the very engines which have lifted them to unjust dominion."

He warned about "the insidious wiles of foreign influence" and the dangers of "ambitious, corrupted, or deluded citizens" who might devote themselves to a favorite foreign nation in order "to betray or sacrifice the interests" of America.

And, finally, Washington warned of the "continual mischiefs of the spirit of party," which are given to creating strife through "ill-founded jealousies and false alarms," and the perils that factionalism (East versus West, North versus South, state versus federal) posed to the unity of the country. Citizens, he said, must indignantly frown "upon the first dawning of every attempt to alienate any portion of our country from the rest, or to enfeeble the sacred ties which now link together the various parts."

America's founding generation spoke frequently of the "common good." Washington reminded citizens of their "common concerns" and "common interests" and the "common cause" they had all fought for in the Revolution. And Thomas Jefferson spoke in his inaugural address of the young country uniting "in common efforts for the common good." A common purpose and a shared sense of reality mattered because they bound the disparate states and regions together, and they remain essential for conducting a national conversation. Especially today in a country where President Trump and Russian and alt-right trolls are working to incite the very factionalism Washington warned us about, trying to inflame divisions between people over racial, ethnic, and religious lines, between red states and blue states, between small towns and big cities.

There are no easy remedies, but it's essential that citizens defy the cynicism and resignation that autocrats and power-hungry politicians depend upon to subvert resistance. The inspiring students who survived the Parkland, Florida, massacre have done just that, rejecting the fatalism of many of their elders; by turning their grief into action, they are changing the national dialogue and leading the charge to get real gun control measures enacted that could help prevent others from suffering the terror and loss they experienced.

At the same time, citizens must look to—and protect—the institutions the founders created as pillars to uphold the roof of democracy: the three branches of government—executive, legislative, and judicial—meant to serve as "reciprocal checks," in

Washington's words, on one another; and the other two foundation stones of democracy that the founders agreed were crucial for creating an informed public that could wisely choose its leaders: education and a free and independent press.

Jefferson wrote that because the young republic was predicated on the proposition "that man may be governed by reason and truth," our "first object should therefore be, to leave open to him all the avenues to truth. The most effectual hitherto found, is the freedom of the press. It is therefore, the first shut up by those who fear the investigation of their actions."

"I hold it, therefore, certain," Jefferson went on, "that to open the doors of truth, and to fortify the habit of testing everything by reason, are the most effectual manacles we can rivet on the hands of our successors to prevent their manacling the people with their own consent."

Madison, somewhat more succinctly, put it like this: "A popular Government, without popular information, or the means of acquiring it, is but a Prologue to a Farce or a Tragedy; or perhaps both." Without commonly agreed-upon facts—not Republican facts and Democratic facts; not the alternative facts of today's silo-world—there can be no rational debate over policies, no substantive means of evaluating candidates for political office, and no way to hold elected officials accountable to the people. Without truth, democracy is hobbled. The founders recognized this, and those seeking democracy's survival must recognize it today.

NOTES

INTRODUCTION

11   **"The ideal subject"**: Hannah Arendt, *The Origins of Totalitarianism* (New York: Harcourt, 1973), 474.

12   **the "danger flags"**: Margaret Atwood, "My Hero: George Orwell," *Guardian*, Jan. 18, 2013.

12   **"The historian knows how"**: Hannah Arendt, "Lying in Politics," in *Crises of the Republic* (New York: Harcourt, 1972), 6.

13   **"diminishing role of facts"**: Jennifer Kavanagh and Michael D. Rich, *Truth Decay: An Initial Exploration of the Diminishing Role of Facts and Analysis in American Public Life* (Rand Corporation, 2018).

13   **2,140 false or misleading claims:** Glenn Kessler and Meg Kelly, "President Trump Made 2,140 False or Misleading Claims in His First Year," *Washington Post*, Jan. 10, 2018.

14   **False claims about the U.K.'s:** Anoosh Chakelian, "Boris Johnson Resurrects the Leave Campaign's £350M for NHS Fantasy," *New Statesman*, Sept. 16, 2017.

14   **"There is no such thing"**: Pope Francis, "Message of His Holiness Pope Francis for World Communications Day," Jan. 24, 2018, http://w2.vatican.va/content/francesco/en/messages/communications/documents/papa-francesco_20180124_messaggio-comunicazioni-sociali.html.

14   **"one of the biggest challenges"**: Jessica Estepa and Gregory Korte, "Obama Tells David Letterman: People No Longer Agree on What Facts Are," *USA Today*, Jan. 12, 2018.

14   **"2017 was a year"**: "Read Sen. Jeff Flake's Speech Criticizing Trump," *CNN Politics*, Jan. 17, 2018.

15   **five billion dollars in free campaign coverage:** Philip Bump, "Assessing a Clinton Argument That the Media Helped to Elect Trump," *Washington Post*, Sept. 12, 2017.

16   **a dozen Diet Cokes a day:** Maggie Haberman, Glenn Thrush, and Peter Baker, "Inside Trump's Hour-by-Hour Battle for Self-Preservation," *New York Times*, Dec. 9, 2017.

16   **It is unlikely that a candidate:** David Barstow, "Donald Trump's Deals Rely on Being Creative with the Truth," *New York Times*, July 16, 2016.

17   **"Everyone is entitled":** "An American Original," *Vanity Fair*, Nov. 2010.

19   **"We can debate policies":** Sally Yates, "Who Are We as a Country? Time to Decide," *USA Today*, Dec. 19, 2017.

1. THE DECLINE AND FALL OF REASON

21   **"This is an apple":** youtube.com/watch?v=IxuuIPcQ9_I.

22   **"spring up amongst us":** Abraham Lincoln, "The Perpetuation of Our Political Institutions," Address Before the Young Men's Lyceum of Springfield, Ill., Jan. 27, 1838, abraham lincolnonline.org.

22   **"a man unprincipled":** Alexander Hamilton, "Objections and Answers Respecting the Administration of the Government," Aug. 18, 1792, founders.archives.gov.

23   **"progress is neither automatic":** Martin Luther King Jr., *Stride Toward Freedom*, in *A Testament of Hope: The Essential Writings and Speeches of Martin Luther King Jr.*, ed. James M. Washington (San Francisco: HarperCollins, 1991), 472.

23   **"can constantly remake ourselves":** Barack Obama, "What I See in Lincoln's Eyes," CNN, June 28, 2005.

23   **"experiment entrusted to the hands":** George Washington, Inaugural Address, Apr. 30, 1789.

23   **"the indigenous American berserk":** Philip Roth, *American Pastoral* (New York: Vintage, 1988), 86.

23   **"heated exaggeration":** Richard Hofstadter, *The Paranoid*

Style in American Politics, and Other Essays (1965; New York: Vintage, 2008), 3.

24   **"a nation, a culture":** Ibid., 4.

24   **"Have you no sense":** "McCarthy-Welch Exchange," June 9, 1954, americanrhetoric.com.

24   **"the State Department harbors":** McCarthy to Truman, Feb. 11, 1950, telegram, archives.gov.

24   **"episodic waves":** Hofstadter, *Paranoid Style in American Politics,* 39.

24   **The anti-Catholic, anti-immigrant:** *Encyclopaedia Britannica,* s.v. "Know-Nothing Party."

25   **"America has been largely taken":** Hofstadter, *Paranoid Style in American Politics,* 39.

25   **nationalist, anti-immigrant leaders:** Ishaan Tharoor, "Geert Wilders and the Mainstreaming of White Nationalism," *Washington Post,* Mar. 14, 2017; Elisabeth Zerofsky, "Europe's Populists Prepare for a Nationalist Spring," *New Yorker,* Jan. 25, 2017; Jason Horowitz, "Italy's Populists Turn Up the Heat as Anti-Migrant Anger Boils," *New York Times,* Feb. 5, 2018.

26   **quoted, in news articles:** Ed Ballard, "Terror, Brexit, and U.S. Election Have Made 2016 the Year of Yeats," *Wall Street Journal,* Aug. 23, 2016.

26   **"Things fall apart":** William Butler Yeats, "The Second Coming," poetryfoundation.org.

26   **Tea Party paranoids who claimed:** "Tea Party Movement Is Full of Conspiracy Theories," *Newsweek,* Feb. 8, 2010.

26   **According to a 2017 survey:** Ariel Malka and Yphtach Lelkes, "In a New Poll, Half of Republicans Say They Would Support Postponing 2020 Election If Trump Proposed It," *Washington Post,* Aug. 10, 2017.

27   **Another study conducted:** Melissa Healy, "It's More Than the 'Rigged' Election: Voters Across the Political Spectrum Believe in Conspiracy Theories," *Los Angeles Times,* Nov. 3, 2016; Shankar Vedantam, "More Americans Than You Might Think Believe in Conspiracy Theories," NPR, June 4, 2014.

177

27   **Trump, who launched his political:** Eric Bradner, "Trump Praises 9/11 Truther's 'Amazing' Reputation," *CNN Politics,* Dec. 2, 2015.

28   **His former chief strategist:** Maggie Haberman, Michael D. Shear, and Glenn Thrush, "Stephen Bannon Out at the White House After Turbulent Run," *New York Times,* Aug. 18, 2017.

28   **"reads to reinforce":** Haberman, Thrush, and Baker, "Inside Trump's Hour-by-Hour Battle for Self-Preservation."

28   **Because such mentions tend:** Greg Miller, Greg Jaffe, and Philip Rucker, "Doubting the Intelligence, Trump Pursues Putin and Leaves a Russian Threat Unchecked," *Washington Post,* Dec. 14, 2017; Carol D. Leonnig, Shane Harris, and Greg Jaffe, "Breaking with Tradition, Trump Skips President's Written Intelligence Report and Relies on Oral Briefings," *Washington Post,* Feb. 9, 2018.

28   **sources like Breitbart News:** Charlie Warzel and Lam Thuy Vo, "Here's Where Donald Trump Gets His News," *BuzzFeed,* Dec. 3, 2016; Dean Obeidallah, "Trump Talks Judgment, Then Cites National Enquirer," CNN, May 4, 2016.

28   **eight hours a day watching:** Haberman, Thrush, and Baker, "Inside Trump's Hour-by-Hour Battle for Self-Preservation."

28   **"admiring tweets, transcripts":** Alex Thompson, "Trump Gets a Folder Full of Positive News About Himself Twice a Day," *Vice News,* Aug. 9, 2017.

29   **"I'm the only one":** Benjamin Hart, "Trump on Unfilled State Department Jobs: 'I Am the Only One That Matters,'" *New York,* Nov. 3, 2017; Bill Chappell, "'I'm the Only One That Matters,' Trump Says of State Dept. Job Vacancies," *The Two-Way,* NPR, Nov. 3, 2017.

29   **Commonsense policies like:** Lydia Saad, "Americans Widely Support Tighter Regulations on Gun Sales," Gallup, Oct. 17, 2017.

29   **Eighty-seven percent of Americans:** Max Greenwood, "Poll: Nearly 9 in 10 Want DACA Recipients to Stay in US," *Hill,* Jan. 18, 2018.

30 **And 83 percent of Americans:** Harper Neidig, "Poll: 83 Percent of Voters Support Keeping FCC's Net Neutrality Rules," *Hill*, Dec. 12, 2017; Cecilia Kang, "F.C.C. Repeals Net Neutrality Rules," *New York Times*, Dec. 14, 2017.

30 **"addiction to infotainment":** Susan Jacoby, *The Age of American Unreason* (New York: Pantheon, 2008), 307; Farhad Manjoo, *True Enough: Learning to Live in a Post-Fact Society* (Hoboken, N.J.: Wiley, 2008); Andrew Keen, *The Cult of the Amateur: How Today's Internet Is Killing Our Culture* (New York: Doubleday, 2007).

30 **"the popular equation of intellectualism":** Jacoby, *Age of American Unreason*, xviii.

30 **"does a poor job of teaching":** Ibid., 307.

31 **"the persistent and sustained reliance":** Al Gore, *The Assault on Reason* (New York: Penguin Press, 2007), 1.

31 **"America's political reality":** Ibid., 38–39.

31 **Indeed, the Iraq war remains:** Michiko Kakutani, "How Feuds and Failures Affected American Intelligence," *New York Times*, June 18, 2004; Michiko Kakutani, "All the President's Books (Minding History's Whys and Wherefores)," *New York Times*, May 11, 2006; Julian Borger, "The Spies Who Pushed for War," *Guardian*, July 17, 2003; Jason Vest and Robert Dreyfuss, "The Lie Factory," *Mother Jones*, Jan./Feb. 2004; Seymour M. Hersh, "Selective Intelligence," *New Yorker*, May 12, 2003; Michiko Kakutani, "Controversial Reports Become Accepted Wisdom," *New York Times*, Sept. 28, 2004; Dana Milbank and Claudia Deane, "Hussein Link to 9/11 Lingers in Many Minds," *Washington Post*, Sept. 6, 2003.

32 **"something on the order of several":** Kakutani, "All the President's Books."

32 **"A cakewalk":** Ken Adelman, "Cakewalk in Iraq," *Washington Post*, Feb. 13, 2002.

33 **"pasting feathers together":** Michiko Kakutani, "From Planning to Warfare to Occupation, How Iraq Went Wrong," *New York Times*, July 25, 2006.

33   **Although Trump frequently criticized:** Eugene Kiely, "Donald Trump and the Iraq War," FactCheck.org, Feb. 19, 2016.

33   **"deconstruction of the administrative state":** Philip Rucker and Robert Costa, "Bannon Vows a Daily Fight for 'Deconstruction of the Administrative State,'" *Washington Post,* Feb. 23, 2017.

34   **crucial role of ambassador:** Victor Cha, "Giving North Korea a 'Bloody Nose' Carries a Huge Risk to Americans," *Washington Post,* Jan. 30, 2018.

34   **world confidence in U.S. leadership:** Bill Chappell, "World's Regard for U.S. Leadership Hits Record Low in Gallup Poll," NPR, Jan. 19, 2018; Laura Smith-Spark, "US Slumps in Global Leadership Poll After Trump's 1st Year," CNN, Jan. 18, 2018.

35   **"the wisdom of the crowd":** Michiko Kakutani, "The Cult of the Amateur," *New York Times,* June 29, 2007.

35   **"every opinion on any matter":** Tom Nichols, *The Death of Expertise: The Campaign Against Established Knowledge and Why It Matters* (New York: Oxford University Press, 2017), 20.

35   **"If citizens do not bother":** Ibid., 11.

36   **Unqualified judges and agency heads:** Carlos Ballesteros, "Trump Is Nominating Unqualified Judges at an Unprecedented Rate," *Newsweek,* Nov. 17, 2017; Paul Waldman, "Donald Trump Has Assembled the Worst Cabinet in American History," *The Plum Line* (blog), *Washington Post,* Jan. 19, 2017; Travis Waldron and Daniel Marans, "Donald Trump's Cabinet Is on Track to Be the Least Experienced in Modern History," *Huffington Post,* Nov. 24, 2016.

36   **Rick Perry, who was famous:** Tom DiChristopher, "Trump Once Again Seeks to Slash Funding for Clean Energy in 2019 Budget," CNBC, Jan. 31, 2018.

36   **the new EPA head, Scott Pruitt:** Brady Dennis, "Scott Pruitt, Longtime Adversary of EPA, Confirmed to Lead the Agency," *Washington Post,* Feb. 17, 2017; Umair Irfan, "Scott Pruitt Is Slowly Strangling the EPA," *Vox,* Jan. 30, 2018.

36   **Congressional Budget Office:** Alan Rappeport, "C.B.O. Head, Who Prizes Nonpartisanship, Finds Work Under G.O.P. Attack," *New York Times,* June 19, 2017; Steven Rattner, "The Boring Little Budget Office That Trump Hates," *New York Times,* Aug. 22, 2017.

37   **"science-based" and "evidence-based":** Lena H. Sun and Juliet Eilperin, "CDC Gets List of Forbidden Words: Fetus, Transgender, Diversity," *Washington Post,* Dec. 15, 2017.

37   **"the empirical method of thought":** George Orwell, *1984* (New York: Harcourt, Brace, 1949), 193.

38   **In addition to announcing:** Lisa Friedman, "Syria Joins Paris Climate Accord, Leaving Only U.S. Opposed," *New York Times,* Nov. 7, 2017.

38   **the Trump administration vowed:** Lisa Friedman, "Expect Environmental Battles to Be 'Even More Significant' in 2018," *New York Times,* Jan. 5, 2018.

38   **Scientists were dismissed:** "President Trump's War on Science," *New York Times,* Sept. 9, 2017; "Attacks on Science," Union of Concerned Scientists, ucsusa.org; Tanya Lewis, "A Year of Trump: Science Is a Major Casualty in the New Politics of Disruption," *Scientific American,* Dec. 14, 2017; Joel Achenbach and Lena H. Sun, "Trump Budget Seeks Huge Cuts to Science and Medical Research, Disease Prevention," *Washington Post,* May 23, 2017; Julia Belluz, "The GOP Tax Plan Would Blow a Hole in American Science," *Vox,* Dec. 11, 2017.

38   **The EPA alone was facing:** Brady Dennis, "Trump Budget Seeks 23 Percent Cut at EPA, Eliminating Dozens of Programs," *Washington Post,* Feb. 12, 2018.

38   **In April 2017, the March for Science:** "Marchers Around the World Tell Us Why They're Taking to the Streets for Science," *Science,* Apr. 13, 2017.

39   **British scientists worry about:** "How Will Leaving the EU Affect Universities and Research?," *Brexit Means . . .* (podcast), *Guardian,* Sept. 13, 2017.

39   **"I liken the attacks on science":** "Marchers Around the

World Tell Us Why They're Taking to the Streets for Science."

39   **"its very opposite, terror"**: Stefan Zweig, *The World of Yesterday* (New York: Viking Press, 1943), loc. 5297, 346, Kindle.

40   **"the transmission of the human word"**: Ibid., 419, 425, 924.

41   **"We had a passion"**: Ibid., 403, 5352.

41   **"The few among writers"**: Ibid., 5378, 5586.

41   **"preached their gospel"**: Ibid., 1269, 5400.

42   **"They practiced their method"**: Ibid., 2939.

42   **"put through by force"**: Ibid., 5378.

2. THE NEW CULTURE WARS

43   **The death of objectivity:** David Lehman, *Signs of the Times: Deconstruction and the Fall of Paul de Man* (New York: Poseidon Press, 1991), 75. See also Michiko Kakutani, "Bending the Truth in a Million Little Ways," *New York Times*, Jan. 17, 2006.

43   **"a kaleidoscope of information"**: David Foster Wallace, "Host: Deep into the Mercenary World of Take-No-Prisoners Political Talk Radio," *Atlantic*, Apr. 2005.

44   **The Republican Party:** Stephen Collinson and Jeremy Diamond, "Trump Again at War with 'Deep State' Justice Department," *CNN Politics*, Jan. 2, 2018.

45   **"We're trying to disrupt"**: Donald J. Trump, "Remarks at a Rally at Waukesha County Expo Center in Waukesha, Wisconsin," Sept. 28, 2016. Online by Gerhard Peters and John T. Woolley, *The American Presidency Project*, presidency.ucsb.edu/ws/index.php?pid=119201.

45   **"failed and corrupt political establishment"**: Ben Illing, "Trump Ran as a Populist. He's Governing as an Elitist. He's Not the First," *Vox*, June 23, 2017.

46   **"Look, I read postmodernist"**: Andrew Marantz, "Trolls for Trump," *New Yorker*, Oct. 31, 2016.

48   **"seen as no more than"**: Christopher Butler, *Postmodernism* (New York: Oxford University Press, 2002), 15.

49   **"resisted the cultural changes"**: Andrew Hartman, *A War*

for the Soul of America: A History of the Culture Wars (Chicago: University of Chicago Press, 2015), 285.

50 **"the final form of human government"**: Ishaan Tharoor, "Fukuyama's 'Future of History': Is Liberal Democracy Doomed?," *Time*, Feb. 8, 2012.

50 **"with populist and nationalist forces"**: Freedom House, *Freedom in the World 2017*, freedomhouse.org.

50 **"a slow erosion"**: Ishaan Tharoor, "The Man Who Declared the 'End of History' Fears for Democracy's Future," *Washington Post*, Feb. 9, 2017.

51 **And Trump, as both candidate**: Jasmine C. Lee and Kevin Quealy, "The 425 People, Places, and Things Donald Trump Has Insulted on Twitter: A Complete List," *New York Times*, Jan. 3, 2018.

51 **Russian trolls used an impostor Facebook account**: Donie O'Sullivan, "Russian Trolls Created Facebook Events Seen by More Than 300,000 Users," CNN, Jan. 26, 2018.

52 **"all these things"**: William J. Barber and Jonathan Wilson-Hartgrove, "Evangelicals Defend Trump's Alleged Marital Infidelity. But His Infidelity to America Is Worse," NBC News, Jan. 30, 2018.

52 **Tony Perkins, president**: Jennifer Hansler, "Conservative Evangelical Leader: Trump Gets a 'Mulligan' on His Behavior," CNN, Jan. 23, 2018.

52 **"commitment was understood"**: Allan Bloom, *The Closing of the American Mind* (New York: Simon & Schuster, 1987), 314.

53 **"it is not only futile"**: Gertrude Himmelfarb, *On Looking into the Abyss: Untimely Thoughts on Culture and Society* (New York: Knopf, 1994), 135.

53 **"knowledge about the past"**: Joyce Appleby, Lynn Hunt, and Margaret Jacob, *Telling the Truth About History* (New York: W. W. Norton, 1994), 8.

54 **"The postmodern view fit well"**: Shawn Otto, *The War on Science: Who's Waging It, Why It Matters, What We Can Do About It* (Minneapolis: Milkweed, 2016), 180–81.

54 **"Atmospheric CO_2 is the same"**: Ibid., 177.

55   **"What is peculiar to our own age"**: George Orwell, "Looking Back on the Spanish War," *A Collection of Essays* (New York: Houghton Mifflin Harcourt, 1981), 199.

56   **"the potential to alter"**: Deborah E. Lipstadt, *Denying the Holocaust: The Growing Assault on Truth and Memory* (New York: Free Press, 1993), loc. 19, Kindle. See also Michiko Kakutani, "When History Is a Casualty," *New York Times,* Apr. 30, 1993.

57   **As David Lehman**: Michiko Kakutani, "The Pro-Nazi Past of a Leading Literary Critic," *New York Times,* Feb. 19, 1991.

57   **De Man, a professor at Yale**: Jon Wiener, "Deconstructing de Man," *Nation,* Jan. 9, 1988; Robert Alter, "Paul de Man Was a Total Fraud," *New Republic,* Apr. 5, 2014; Evelyn Barish, *The Double Life of Paul de Man* (New York: Liveright, 2014).

57   **A very different portrait**: Barish, *Double Life of Paul de Man;* Jennifer Schuessler, "Revisiting a Scholar Unmasked by Scandal," *New York Times,* Mar. 9, 2014; Louis Menand, "The de Man Case," *New Yorker,* Mar. 24, 2014.

58   **The most shocking news**: Lehman, *Signs of the Times,* 163–64.

58   **"we are determined to forbid"**: Ibid., 180.

58   **"Jewish writers have always"**: Kakutani, "Pro-Nazi Past of a Leading Literary Critic"; Paul de Man, "The Jews in Contemporary Literature," *Le Soir,* Mar. 4, 1941, reprinted in Martin McQuillan, *Paul de Man* (New York: Routledge, 2001).

59   **"considerations of the actual"**: Kakutani, "Pro-Nazi Past of a Leading Literary Critic."

59   **More disturbing still**: Lehman, *Signs of the Times,* 137, 158, 234.

59   **"one of detached mockery"**: Ibid., 238, 239, 243, 267.

60   **"have to take each word"**: David Brunnstrom, "Ahead of Trump Meeting, Abe Told Not to Take Campaign Rhetoric Literally," Reuters, Nov. 15, 2016.

60   **"You guys took everything"**: Jonah Goldberg, "Take Trump Seriously but Not Literally? How, Exactly?," *Los Angeles Times*, Dec. 6, 2016.

3. "MOI" AND THE RISE OF SUBJECTIVITY

61   **"Our subjectivity is so completely"**: James Mottram, "Spike Jonze Interview: *Her* Is My 'Boy Meets Computer' Movie," *Independent*, Jan. 31, 2014.

61   **"ethic of self-preservation"**: Christopher Lasch, *The Culture of Narcissism: American Life in an Age of Diminishing Expectations* (New York: W. W. Norton, 1979), 51, xiii, 239.

62   **"intense feelings of rage"**: Ibid., 36–38.

62   **"remaking, remodeling, elevating"**: Tom Wolfe, "The 'Me' Decade and the Third Great Awakening," *New York*, Aug. 23, 1976.

63   **"the preening self"**: Tim Wu, *The Attention Merchants: The Epic Scramble to Get Inside Our Heads* (New York: Alfred A. Knopf, 2016), 315.

63   **"My net worth fluctuates"**: David A. Fahrenthold and Robert O'Harrow Jr., "Trump: A True Story," *Washington Post*, Aug. 10, 2016; Kiran Khalid, "Trump: I'm Worth Whatever I Feel," CNNMoney.com, Apr. 21, 2011.

63   **"I believe that he feels"**: Scott Horsley, "Trump: Putin Again Denied Interfering in Election and 'I Really Believe' He Means It," *The Two-Way*, NPR, Nov. 11, 2017.

64   **"I understand your view"**: Transcripts, CNN, July 22, 2016, transcripts.cnn.com/TRANSCRIPTS/1607/22/nday.06 .html.

65   **"small private societies"**: Alexis de Tocqueville, *Democracy in America* (New York: Vintage, 1990), 215, 319, 318, 321.

66   **Norman Vincent Peale:** James Barron, "Overlooked Influences on Donald Trump: A Famous Minister and His Church," *New York Times*, Sept. 5, 2016; Tom Gjelten, "How Positive Thinking, Prosperity Gospel Define Donald Trump's Faith Outlook," NPR, Aug. 3, 2016.

66 **"Any fact facing us":** Tamara Keith, "Trump Crowd Size Estimate May Involve 'the Power of Positive Thinking,'" NPR, Jan. 22, 2017.

66 **Ayn Rand, also admired:** Mackenzie Weinger, "7 Pols Who Praised Ayn Rand," *Politico,* Apr. 26, 2012.

66 **over the years, *The Fountainhead*:** Kirsten Powers, "Donald Trump's 'Kinder, Gentler' Version," *USA Today,* Apr. 11, 2016.

66 **"highest moral purpose":** Jonathan Freedland, "The New Age of Ayn Rand: How She Won Over Trump and Silicon Valley," *Guardian,* Apr. 10, 2017.

67 **"a kind of embarrassment":** Philip Roth, "Writing American Fiction," *Commentary,* Mar. 1, 1961.

68 **"head out into this wild":** Tom Wolfe, "Stalking the Billion-Footed Beast: A Literary Manifesto for the New Social Novel," *Harper's,* Nov. 1989.

68 **"depends on what the meaning":** "From the Starr Referral: Clinton's Grand Jury Testimony, Part 4," *Washington Post,* washingtonpost.com/wp-srv/politics/special/clinton /stories/bctest092198_4.htm.

68 **"the sheer fact of self":** Roth, "Writing American Fiction."

69 **"wholly fabricated or wildly embellished":** Kakutani, "Bending the Truth in a Million Little Ways."

69–70 **"most of what":** Laura Barton, "The Man Who Rewrote His Life," *Guardian,* Sept. 15, 2006.

70 **"spread in tandem":** Adam Begley, "The I's Have It: Duke's '*Moi*' Critics Expose Themselves," *Lingua Franca,* Mar./ Apr. 1994.

71 **In her 1996 book:** Michiko Kakutani, "Opinion vs. Reality in an Age of Pundits," *New York Times,* Jan. 28, 1994; Michiko Kakutani, "Fear of Fat as the Bane of Modernism," *New York Times,* Mar. 12, 1996.

71 **Personal stories or agendas:** Michiko Kakutani, "A Biographer Who Claims a License to Blur Reality," *New York Times,* Oct. 2, 1999.

72 **"understand the first thing":** Ibid.

72–73 **"feeling of tenderness"**: Michiko Kakutani, "Taking Sides in Polemics over Plath," *New York Times*, Apr. 5, 1994; Janet Malcolm, *The Silent Woman* (New York: Knopf, 1994), loc. 67, 32, Kindle.

73 **"Teach both," some argued**: Sam Boyd, "Sarah Palin on Teaching Intelligent Design in Schools," *American Prospect*, Aug. 29, 2008; Massimo Pigliucci, "Is Sarah Palin a Creationist?," *LiveScience*, Sept. 1, 2008.

73 **"Teach the controversy"**: John Timmer, "Ohio School District Has 'Teach the Controversy' Evolution Lesson Plan," *Ars Technica*, May 18, 2016.

73 **"some very fine people"**: Rosie Gray, "Trump Defends White-Nationalist Protesters: 'Some Very Fine People on Both Sides,'" *Atlantic*, Aug. 15, 2017; Mark Landler, "Trump Resurrects His Claim That Both Sides Share Blame in Charlottesville Violence," *New York Times*, Sept. 14, 2017; Sonam Sheth, "Trump Equates Confederate Generals Robert E. Lee and Stonewall Jackson with George Washington in Bizarre Press Conference," *Business Insider*, Aug. 15, 2017; Dan Merica, "Trump Condemns 'Hatred, Bigotry, and Violence on Many Sides' in Charlottesville," *CNN Politics*, Aug. 13, 2017.

74 **As Naomi Oreskes**: Naomi Oreskes and Erik M. Conway, *Merchants of Doubt* (New York: Bloomsbury Press, 2010), 6.

74 **"Doubt is our product"**: Ibid., 34.

74 **The strategy, essentially, was this**: Ibid., 6–7, 217.

75 **the "Tobacco Strategy"**: Ibid., 6, 215.

75 **This false equivalence**: Alister Doyle, "Scientists Say United on Global Warming, at Odds with Public View," Reuters, May 15, 2013; NASA, "Scientific Consensus: Earth's Climate Is Warming," climate.nasa.gov/scientific-consensus/; Justin Fox, "97 Percent Consensus on Climate Change? It's Complicated," *Bloomberg*, June 15, 2017.

75 **"undue attention to marginal"**: David Robert Grimes, "Impartial Journalism Is Laudable. But False Balance Is Dangerous," *Guardian*, Nov. 8, 2016.

75   **Or, as a headline:** Sarah Knapton, "BBC Staff Told to Stop Inviting Cranks on to Science Programmes," *Telegraph*, July 4, 2014.

76   **"Like many people watching":** Christiane Amanpour, speech on receiving the Burton Benjamin Memorial Award, Nov. 22, 2016, cpj.org.

4. THE VANISHING OF REALITY

77   **"Do I want to interfere":** Philip K. Dick, "The Electric Ant," in *Selected Stories of Philip K. Dick* (New York: Houghton Mifflin Harcourt, 2013), Kindle, p. 384 of 467.

77   **at a time when nineteen kids:** Christopher Ingraham, "19 Kids Are Shot Every Day in the United States," *Washington Post*, June 20, 2017.

78   **"It stupefies, it sickens":** Roth, "Writing American Fiction."

79   **"perception is reality":** Simon Kelner, "Perception Is Reality: The Facts Won't Matter in Next Year's General Election," *Independent*, Oct. 30, 2014; Roxie Salamon-Abrams, "Echoes of History? A Lesson Plan About the Recent Rise of Europe's Far-Right Parties," *New York Times*, Apr. 19, 2017.

79   **But Atwater's cold-blooded use:** Lawrence Freedman, "Reagan's Southern Strategy Gave Rise to the Tea Party," *Salon*, Oct. 27, 2013.

80   **Depicting America as a country:** Eugene Kiely, Lori Robertson, and Robert Farley, "President Trump's Inaugural Address," FactCheck.org, Jan. 20, 2017; Chris Nichols, "Mostly True: Undocumented Immigrants Less Likely to Commit Crimes Than U.S. Citizens," PolitiFact California, Aug. 3, 2017; Akhila Satish, "The Nobel Laureate Exclusion Act: No Future Geniuses Need Apply," *Wall Street Journal*, Sept. 14, 2017; Rani Molla, "The Top U.S. Tech Companies Founded by Immigrants Are Now Worth Nearly $4 Trillion," *Recode*, Jan. 12, 2018; "Fact Check:

Donald Trump's Republican Convention Speech, Annotated," NPR, July 21, 2016.

81   **Long before he entered politics:** Vivian Yee, "Donald Trump's Math Takes His Towers to Greater Heights," *New York Times,* Nov. 1, 2016; Marc Fisher and Will Hobson, "Donald Trump Masqueraded as Publicist to Brag About Himself," *Washington Post,* May 13, 2016; David Barstow, "Donald Trump's Deals Rely on Being Creative with the Truth," *New York Times,* July 16, 2016; Fahrenthold and O'Harrow, "Trump: A True Story."

81   **He spent years as a real-estate developer:** Aaron Williams and Anu Narayanswamy, "How Trump Has Made Millions by Selling His Name," *Washington Post,* Jan. 25, 2017; "10 Donald Trump Business Failures," *Time,* Oct. 11, 2016.

81–82   **"planned, planted, or incited":** Daniel J. Boorstin, *The Image* (New York: Macmillan, 1987), 11.

82   **for his "well-knownness":** Ibid., 65.

82   **would even host a show:** Laura Bradley, "Trump Bashes Schwarzenegger's *Celebrity Apprentice,* Forgets He Still Produces It," *Vanity Fair,* Jan. 6, 2017.

82   **"prince of humbugs":** Boorstin, *Image,* 209–11.

82   **Much the way images:** Ibid., 241, 212.

83   **"desert of the real":** https://en.wikiquote.org/wiki/Jean _Baudrillard; *Stanford Encyclopedia of Philosophy,* s.v. "Jean Baudrillard"; Jean Baudrillard, *Simulacra and Simulation* (Ann Arbor: University of Michigan Press, 1994).

83   **"a secret society of astronomers":** Jorge Luis Borges, *Ficciones* (New York: Grove Press, 1962), loc. 21–22, 34, Kindle.

84   **"Reality gave ground":** Ibid., 33.

85   **"If there is something comforting":** Thomas Pynchon, *Gravity's Rainbow* (New York: Viking Press, 1973), loc. 434, Kindle.

85   **In a 2016 documentary:** Brandon Harris, "Adam Curtis's Essential Counterhistories," *New Yorker,* Nov. 3, 2016.

86   **"red-pilling the normies":** Alice Marwick and Rebecca

Lewis, "The Online Radicalization We're Not Talking About," *Select All*, May 18, 2017.

86   **study on online disinformation:** Alice Marwick and Rebecca Lewis, *Media Manipulation and Disinformation Online,* Data and Society Research Institute, May 15, 2017.

86   **"once groups have been red-pilled":** Marwick and Lewis, "Online Radicalization We're Not Talking About."

87   **"it's a surprisingly short leap":** Ibid.

87   **a lot of fake news:** BBC Trending, "The Saga of 'Pizzagate': The Fake Story That Shows How Conspiracy Theories Spread," BBC News, Dec. 2, 2016.

87   **Reddit can be a useful testing ground:** Ali Breland, "Warner Sees Reddit as Potential Target for Russian Influence," *Hill,* Sept. 27, 2017; Roger McNamee, "How to Fix Facebook—Before It Fixes Us," *Washington Monthly,* Jan./Feb./Mar. 2018.

88   **"asymmetry of passion":** Renee DiResta, "Social Network Algorithms Are Distorting Reality by Boosting Conspiracy Theories," *Fast Company,* May 11, 2016.

5. THE CO-OPTING OF LANGUAGE

89   **"Without clear language":** John le Carré, "Why We Should Learn German," *Guardian,* July 1, 2017.

89   **"We swim in language":** James Carroll, *Practicing Catholic* (Boston: Houghton Mifflin Harcourt, 2009), 302.

89   **"political chaos is connected":** George Orwell, "Politics and the English Language," in *A Collection of Essays by George Orwell* (Garden City, N.Y.: Anchor Books, 1954), 177.

90   **Ministry of Truth:** Orwell, *1984,* Kindle.

90   **characteristics of "wooden language":** Roger Scruton, "Newspeak," in *The Palgrave Macmillan Dictionary of Political Thought,* 3rd ed. (New York: Palgrave Macmillan, 2007); "The Wooden Language," Radio Romania International, old.rri.ro/arh-art.shtml?lang=1&sec=9&art=4166.

90   **Thom identified in a 1987 thesis:** Françoise Thom, *La langue de bois* (Paris: Julliard, 1987).

90 **Mao's Communist Party also adopted:** Ji Fengyuan, *Linguistic Engineering: Language and Politics in Mao's China* (Honolulu: University of Hawaii Press, 2003); Perry Link, "Mao's China: The Language Game," *NYR Daily*, May 15, 2015.

90 **One of history's most detailed:** Timothy Snyder, "A New Look at Civilian Life in Europe Under Hitler," review of *An Iron Wind: Europe Under Hitler*, by Peter Fritzsche, *New York Times*, Nov. 22, 2016.

91 **"tiny doses of arsenic":** Victor Klemperer, *The Language of the Third Reich* (New York: Bloomsbury, 2013), 12, 15.

91 **Klemperer didn't think Hitler:** Ibid., 54–55, 30, 118, 44–45.

92 **"a threatening and repulsive":** Ibid., 60–62, 5, 101–3.

92 **"literally fixed the essential features":** Ibid., 19.

93 **"finished off the biggest elephants":** Ibid., 222, 227, 223, 224, 228.

94 **"WAR IS PEACE":** Orwell, *1984* (New York: Signet Classics, 1950), 16.

95 **"the single greatest witch hunt":** Rebecca Savransky, "Trump: 'You Are Witnessing the Single Greatest WITCH HUNT in American Political History,'" *Hill*, June 15, 2017; Michael Finnegan, "Trump Attacks on Russia Investigation Threaten U.S. Democracy, Authors Say," *Los Angeles Times*, Feb. 6, 2018; Anne Gearan, "Trump's Attacks on Justice and FBI Echo Election Claims of a 'Rigged System,'" *Washington Post*, Feb. 2, 2018.

95 **Trump has the perverse habit:** Jessica Estepa, "It's Not Just 'Rocket Man.' Trump Has Long History of Nicknaming His Foes," *USA Today*, Sept. 21, 2017; Theodore Schleifer and Jeremy Diamond, "Clinton Says Trump Leading 'Hate Movement'; He Calls Her a 'Bigot,'" *CNN Politics*, Aug. 25, 2016; "Excerpts from Trump's Interview with the Times," *New York Times*, Dec. 28, 2017.

95 **"two mutually contradictory meanings":** Orwell, *1984*, 212.

96 **the "largest audience":** Linda Qiu, "Donald Trump Had Biggest Inaugural Crowd Ever? Metrics Don't Show It," *PolitiFact*, Jan. 21, 2017.

96   **"to assert power over truth"**: Masha Gessen, "The Putin Paradigm," *NYR Daily*, Dec. 13, 2016.

97   **"It is not merely that speeches"**: Orwell, *1984*, 213.

97   **within days of Trump's inauguration:** Oliver Milman and Sam Morris, "Trump Is Deleting Climate Change, One Site at a Time," *Guardian*, May 14, 2017; Brian Kahn, "The EPA Has Started to Remove Obama-Era Information," *Climate Central*, Feb. 2, 2017; Leila Miller, "As 'Climate Change' Fades from Government Sites, a Struggle to Archive Data," *Frontline*, Dec. 8, 2017.

97   **Some of their fears were realized:** Megan Cerullo, "EPA Removes Climate Change Page from Website to Reflect New 'Priorities' Under President Trump," *New York Daily News*, Apr. 29, 2017; Bill McKibben, "The Trump Administration's Solution to Climate Change: Ban the Term," *Guardian*, Aug. 8, 2017; Oliver Milman, "US Federal Department Is Censoring Use of Term 'Climate Change,' Emails Reveal," *Guardian*, Aug. 7, 2017; Lydia Smith, "Trump Administration Deletes Mention of 'Climate Change' from Environmental Protection Agency's Website," *Independent*, Oct. 21, 2017; Michael Collins, "EPA Removes Climate Change Data, Other Scientific Information from Website," *USA Today*, Apr. 29, 2017; Oliver Milman and Sam Morris, "Trump Is Deleting Climate Change, One Site at a Time," *Guardian*, May 14, 2017.

98   **USDA employees were informed:** Valerie Volcovici and P. J. Huffstutter, "Trump Administration Seeks to Muzzle U.S. Agency Employees," Reuters, Jan. 24, 2017; Lisa Friedman, "E.P.A. Cancels Talk on Climate Change by Agency Scientists," *New York Times*, Oct. 22, 2017; Dan Merica and Dana Bash, "Trump Admin Tells National Park Service to Halt Tweets," *CNN Politics*, Jan. 23, 2017.

99   **"He wants to see":** Michiko Kakutani, "Donald Trump's Chilling Language, and the Fearsome Power of Words," *Vanity Fair*, Jan. 21, 2017.

99   **He is equally nonchalant about spelling:** Aidan Quigley, "Make America Spell Again? 25 of Donald Trump's Twit-

ter Spelling Errors," *Newsweek,* June 25, 2017; Jennifer Calfas, "Trump's Official Inauguration Poster Has Glaring Typo," *Hill,* Feb. 12, 2017; Eli Rosenberg, "'State of the Uniom': Misspelled Tickets to President Trump's First Address Require a Reprint," *Washington Post,* Jan. 29, 2018.

100   **Trump's tweets have been deemed official:** Elizabeth Landers, "White House: Trump's Tweets Are 'Official Statements,'" *CNN Politics,* June 6, 2017; Matthew Weaver, Robert Booth, and Ben Jacobs, "Theresa May Condemns Trump's Retweets of UK Far-Right Leader's Anti-Muslim Videos," *Guardian,* Nov. 29, 2017.

101   **His rants against journalism:** Steven Erlanger, "'Fake News,' Trump's Obsession, Is Now a Cudgel for Strongmen," *New York Times,* Dec. 12, 2017; Anne Applebaum, "The 'Trump Effect' Will Help Authoritarians Around the World," *Washington Post,* May 4, 2016; "Record Number of Journalists Jailed as Turkey, China, Egypt Pay Scant Price for Repression," Committee to Protect Journalists, Dec. 13, 2017.

102   **"the limits of what the public":** Ruth Ben-Ghiat, "An American Authoritarian," *Atlantic,* Aug. 10, 2016.

102   **"Mussolini did not have any philosophy":** Umberto Eco, "Ur-fascism," *New York Review of Books,* June 22, 1995.

103   **"I'm with you":** "Full Text: Donald Trump 2016 RNC Draft Speech Transcript," *Politico,* July 21, 2016.

6. FILTERS, SILOS, AND TRIBES

105   **"We're all islands":** Rudyard Kipling, *The Light That Failed,* in *Selected Works of Rudyard Kipling* (New York: Collier & Son, 1900), 2:61.

105   **"How can the polls":** Deborah Solomon, "Goodbye (Again), Norma Jean," *New York Times,* Sept. 19, 2004.

106   **A 2016 Pew survey:** Pew Research Center, *Partisanship and Political Animosity in 2016,* June 22, 2016.

106   **It's telling that the old national motto:** David Nakamura and Lisa Rein, "It's 'Very Gold': The Presidential Coin

Undergoes a Trumpian Makeover," *Washington Post*, Dec. 22, 2017.

106 **These growing divides in America:** Bill Bishop, *The Big Sort: Why the Clustering of Like-Minded America Is Tearing Us Apart* (New York: Houghton Mifflin Harcourt, 2008), 130–32, 12.

107 **"As we've lost trust":** Ibid., 216.

107 **"as the parties have come to represent lifestyle":** Ibid., 232.

108 **A 2017 Pew survey:** Pew Research Center, "Sharp Partisan Divisions in Views of National Institutions," July 10, 2017.

108 **"This is not designed":** Ronald Brownstein, *The Second Civil War: How Extreme Partisanship Has Paralyzed Washington and Polarized America* (New York: Penguin Press, 2007), loc. 4247, Kindle.

109 **Hillary Clinton's campaign:** Molly Ball, "Why Hillary Clinton Lost," *Atlantic*, Nov. 15, 2016.

109 **a 2014 Pew survey:** Pew Research Center, "Political Polarization in the American Public," June 12, 2014; Pew Research Center, *Partisanship and Political Animosity in 2016*.

109 **And then there is gerrymandering:** Julian E. Zelizer, "The Power That Gerrymandering Has Brought to Republicans," *Washington Post*, June 17, 2016; Ronald Brownstein, "America, a Year Later," *State: The Digital Magazine from CNN Politics*, Nov. 2017.

110 **"further apart from one another":** Pew Research Center, "Political Polarization in the American Public"; Pew Research Center, *Partisanship and Political Animosity in 2016*.

111 **"the Four Corners of Deceit":** "The Four Corners of Deceit: Prominent Liberal Social Psychologist Made It All Up," *Rush Limbaugh Show*, Apr. 29, 2013.

111 **In the three decades since the FCC:** Dylan Matthews, "Everything You Need to Know About the Fairness Doctrine in One Post," *Washington Post*, Aug. 23, 2011; Yochai Benkler et al., "Study: Breitbart-Led Right-Wing Media Ecosystem Altered Broader Media Agenda," *Columbia Journalism Review*, Mar. 3, 2017; Maggie Haberman and Glenn Thrush, "Bannon in Limbo as Trump Faces Growing Calls

for the Strategist's Ouster," *New York Times,* Aug. 14, 2017; Michael J. de la Merced and Nicholas Fandos, "Fox's Unfamiliar but Powerful Television Rival: Sinclair," *New York Times,* May 3, 2017.

112 **"truth-based content":** John Ziegler, "How Donald Trump's Election Has Helped Me Decide to End My National Radio Show," *Mediaite,* Dec. 18, 2016.

112 **Charlie Sykes observed:** Charles Sykes, "How the Right Lost Its Mind and Embraced Donald Trump," *Newsweek,* Sept. 21, 2017; Charles Sykes, "Charlie Sykes on Where the Right Went Wrong," *New York Times,* Dec. 15, 2016.

112 **A 2017 Harvard study:** Benkler et al., "Study: Breitbart-Led Right-Wing Media Ecosystem Altered Broader Media Agenda"; Alexandra Topping, "'Sweden, Who Would Believe This?' Trump Cites Non-existent Terror Attack," *Guardian,* Feb. 19, 2017; Samantha Schmidt and Lindsey Bever, "Kellyanne Conway Cites 'Bowling Green Massacre' That Never Happened to Defend Travel Ban," *Washington Post,* Feb. 3, 2017.

113 **Trump supporters who booed:** Alexander Nazaryan, "John McCain Cancer Is 'Godly Justice' for Challenging Trump, Alt-Right Claims," *Newsweek,* July 20, 2017.

113 **"The enduring, complicated divides":** Andrew Sullivan, "America Wasn't Built for Humans," *New York,* Sept. 19, 2017.

114 **confirmation bias:** Elizabeth Kolbert, "Why Facts Don't Change Our Minds," *New Yorker,* Feb. 27, 2017.

114 **"does not encourage dissent":** Cass Sunstein, *Going to Extremes: How Like Minds Unite and Divide* (New York: Oxford University Press, 2009), 87.

114 **"the information and views":** Ibid., 4.

115 **"binary tribal world":** Sykes, "How the Right Lost Its Mind and Embraced Donald Trump"; Sykes, "Charlie Sykes on Where the Right Went Wrong."

115 **"In the new Right media culture":** Charles Sykes, *How the Right Lost Its Mind* (New York: St. Martin's Press, 2017), 180.

116 **"With Google personalized"**: Eli Pariser, *The Filter Bubble: What the Internet Is Hiding from You* (New York: Penguin Press, 2011), 3.

117 **"an endless you-loop"**: Ibid., 16.

117 **"If algorithms are going to curate"**: Eli Pariser, "Beware Online 'Filter Bubbles,'" TED2011, ted.com.

7. ATTENTION DEFICIT

119 **"When you want to know"**: William Gibson, *Zero History* (New York: Putnam, 2010), 212.

119 **Tim Berners-Lee:** "History of the Web: Sir Tim Berners-Lee," World Wide Web Foundation.

120 **"The rise of the web"**: Jaron Lanier, *You Are Not a Gadget* (New York: Alfred A. Knopf, 2010), loc. 332–33, Kindle.

121 **"We don't see the forest"**: Nicholas Carr, *The Shallows: What the Internet Is Doing to Our Brains* (New York: W. W. Norton, 2010), 91.

122 **"urge to share was activated"**: Wu, *Attention Merchants*, 320.

122 **"a commons that fostered"**: Ibid., 322.

123 **two-thirds of Americans:** "'Who Shared It?' How Americans Decide What News to Trust on Social Media," American Press Institute, Mar. 20, 2017; Elisa Shearer and Jeffrey Gottfried, "News Use Across Social Media Platforms 2017," Pew Research Center, Sept. 7, 2017.

123 **Fake news is nothing new:** "Yellow Journalism," in *Crucible of Empire: The Spanish-American War,* PBS, pbs.org; Jacob Soll, "The Long and Brutal History of Fake News," *Politico,* Dec. 18, 2016; "Gaius Julius Caesar: The Conquest of Gaul," Livius.org.

123 **man behind the massacre:** Kevin Roose, "After Las Vegas Shooting, Fake News Regains Its Megaphone," *New York Times,* Oct. 2, 2017; Jennifer Medina, "A New Report on the Las Vegas Gunman Was Released. Here Are Some Takeaways," *New York Times,* Jan. 19, 2018.

123   **During the last three months:** Craig Silverman, "This Analysis Shows How Viral Fake Election News Stories Outperformed Real News on Facebook," *BuzzFeed*, Nov. 16, 2016.

124   **A study from Oxford:** Oxford Internet Institute, "Trump Supporters and Extreme Right 'Share Widest Range of Junk News,'" Feb. 6, 2018; Ishaan Tharoor, "'Fake News' and the Trumpian Threat to Democracy," *Washington Post*, Feb. 7, 2018; Shawn Musgrave and Matthew Nussbaum, "Trump Thrives in Areas That Lack Traditional News Outlets," *Politico*, Apr. 8, 2018.

124   **"the monetization and manipulation":** Pierre Omidyar, "6 Ways Social Media Has Become a Direct Threat to Democracy," *Washington Post*, Oct. 9, 2017; Omidyar Group, *Is Social Media a Threat to Democracy?*, Oct. 1, 2017.

124   **"The system is failing":** Olivia Solon, "Tim Berners-Lee on the Future of the Web: 'The System Is Failing,'" *Guardian*, Nov. 15, 2017.

125   **"the level of political discourse":** McNamee, "How to Fix Facebook—Before It Fixes Us"; Nicholas Thompson and Fred Vogelstein, "Inside the Two Years That Shook Facebook—and the World," *Wired*, Feb. 12, 2018.

126   **"We got elected":** Michael Lewis, "Has Anyone Seen the President?," *Bloomberg View*, Feb. 9, 2018.

126   **Trump campaign made shrewd:** Matea Gold and Frances Stead Sellers, "After Working for Trump's Campaign, British Data Firm Eyes New U.S. Government Contracts," *Washington Post*, Feb. 17, 2017; Nicholas Confessore and Danny Hakim, "Data Firm Says 'Secret Sauce' Aided Trump; Many Scoff," *New York Times*, Mar. 6, 2017; Joshua Green and Sasha Issenberg, "Inside the Trump Bunker, with Days to Go," *Bloomberg*, Oct. 27, 2016.

126   **Facebook revealed:** Matthew Rosenberg and Gabriel J.X. Dance, "'You Are the Product': Targeted by Cambridge Analytica on Facebook," *New York Times*, Apr. 8, 2018; Carole Cadwalladr and Emma Graham-Harrison, "Revealed: 50 Million Facebook Profiles Harvested for

Cambridge Analytica in Major Data Breach," *Guardian*, Mar. 17, 2018; Olivia Solon, "Facebook Says Cambridge Analytica May Have Gained 37m More Users' Data," *Guardian*, Apr. 4, 2018.

127   **voter persuasion effort:** Craig Timberg, Karla Adam, and Michael Kranish, "Bannon Oversaw Cambridge Analytica's Collection of Facebook Data, According to Former Employee," *Washington Post*, Mar. 20, 2018; Isobel Thompson, "The Secret History of Steve Bannon and Alexander Nix, Explained," *Vanity Fair*, Mar. 21, 2018.

127   **The Trump campaign's digital director:** Lesley Stahl, "Facebook 'Embeds,' Russia, and the Trump Campaign's Secret Weapon," *60 Minutes*, Oct. 8, 2017.

127   **The campaign also used:** Green and Issenberg, "Inside the Trump Bunker, with Days to Go"; David A. Graham, "Trump's 'Voter Suppression Operation' Targets Black Voters," *Atlantic*, Oct. 27, 2016.

128   **The master manipulators of social media:** Shane Harris, "Russian Hackers Who Compromised DNC Are Targeting the Senate, Company Says," *Washington Post*, Jan. 12, 2018; Raphael Satter, "Inside Story: How Russians Hacked the Democrats' Emails," Associated Press, Nov. 4, 2017; Priyanka Boghani, "How Russia Looks to Gain Through Political Interference," *Frontline*, Dec. 23, 2016; Rick Noack, "Everything We Know So Far About Russian Election Meddling in Europe," *Washington Post*, Jan. 10, 2018; U.S. Senate, Committee on Foreign Relations, *Putin's Asymmetric Assault on Democracy in Russia and Europe: Implications for U.S. National Security*, 115th Cong., 2nd sess., Jan. 10, 2018.

128   **In the case of the American election:** David Ingram, "Facebook Says 126 Million Americans May Have Seen Russia-Linked Political Posts," Reuters, Oct. 30, 2017; Shane Goldmacher, "America Hits New Landmark: 200 Million Registered Voters," *Politico*, Oct. 19, 2016; Scott Shane, "These Are the Ads Russia Bought on Facebook in 2016,"

New York Times, Nov. 1, 2017; Leslie Shapiro, "Anatomy of a Russian Facebook Ad," *Washington Post*, Nov. 1, 2017.

129 **"The strategy is to take a crack":** Craig Timberg et al., "Russian Ads, Now Publicly Released, Show Sophistication of Influence Campaign," *Washington Post*, Nov. 1, 2017.

129 **Reporting from several publications:** Jack Nicas, "How YouTube Drives People to the Internet's Darkest Corners," *Wall Street Journal*, Feb. 7, 2018; Paul Lewis, "'Fiction Is Outperforming Reality': How YouTube's Algorithm Distorts Truth," *Guardian*, Feb. 2, 2018; Jon Swaine, "Twitter Admits Far More Russian Bots Posted on Election Than It Had Disclosed," *Guardian*, Jan. 19, 2018; Philip N. Howard et al., "Social Media, News, and Political Information During the US Election: Was Polarizing Content Concentrated in Swing States?," Computational Propaganda Research Project, Sept. 28, 2017.

130 **Russians had become very adept:** Ben Popken and Kelly Cobiella, "Russian Troll Describes Work in the Infamous Misinformation Factory," NBC News, Nov. 16, 2017; Scott Shane, "The Fake Americans Russia Created to Influence the Election," *New York Times*, Sept. 7, 2017.

130 **When the *Access Hollywood* tape:** Ryan Nakashima and Barbara Ortutay, "Russia Twitter Trolls Deflected Trump Bad News," *USA Today*, Nov. 10, 2017; Issie Lapowsky, "Pro-Kremlin Twitter Trolls Take Aim at Robert Mueller," *Wired*, Jan. 5, 2018.

131 **repeal net neutrality:** Neidig, "Poll: 83 Percent of Voters Support Keeping FCC's Net Neutrality Rules"; Todd Shields, "FCC Got 444,938 Net-Neutrality Comments from Russian Email Addresses," *Bloomberg*, Nov. 29, 2017; "Over Half of Public Comments to FCC on Net Neutrality Appear Fake: Study," Reuters, Nov. 29, 2017; Susan Decker, "FCC Rules Out Delaying Net Neutrality Repeal over Fake Comments," *Bloomberg*, Jan. 5, 2018; Jon Brodkin, "FCC Stonewalled Investigation of Net Neutrality Comment Fraud, NY AG Says," *Ars Technica*,

Nov. 22, 2017; Brian Fung, "FCC Net Neutrality Process 'Corrupted' by Fake Comments and Vanishing Consumer Complaints, Officials Say," *Washington Post*, Nov. 24, 2017; James V. Grimaldi and Paul Overberg, "Millions of People Post Comments on Federal Regulations. Many Are Fake," *Wall Street Journal*, Dec. 12, 2017; James V. Grimaldi and Paul Overberg, "Many Comments Critical of 'Fiduciary' Rule Are Fake," *Wall Street Journal*, Dec. 27, 2017.

132 **"Sometimes, when political parties":** Samantha Bradshaw and Philip N. Howard, "Troops, Trolls, and Troublemakers: A Global Inventory of Organized Social Media Manipulation," Computational Propaganda Research Project, working paper no. 2017.12.

132 **The use of bots:** Omidyar, "6 Ways Social Media Has Become a Direct Threat to Democracy"; Omidyar Group, *Is Social Media a Threat to Democracy?*

132 **Things are only likely to get worse:** Julia Munslow, "Ex-CIA Director Hayden: Russia Election Meddling Was 'Most Successful Covert Operation in History,'" *Yahoo News*, July 21, 2017; Cynthia McFadden, William M. Arkin, and Kevin Monahan, "Russians Penetrated U.S. Voter Systems, Top U.S. Official Says," NBC News, Feb. 8, 2018; Harris, "Russian Hackers Who Compromised DNC Are Targeting the Senate."

133 **Russia already tried to meddle:** Shannon O'Neil, "Don't Let Mexico's Elections Become Putin's Next Target," *Bloomberg View*, Nov. 9, 2017; Jason Horowitz, "Italy, Bracing for Electoral Season of Fake News, Demands Facebook's Help," *New York Times*, Nov. 24, 2017; Yasmeen Serhan, "Italy Scrambles to Fight Misinformation Ahead of Its Elections," *Atlantic*, Feb. 24, 2018; "Italy Warns of Election Threat as Rival Parties Court Russia," ABC News, Feb. 21, 2018.

133 **Technological developments are likely:** Olivia Solon, "The Future of Fake News: Don't Believe Everything You Read, See, or Hear," *Guardian*, July 26, 2017; Cade Metz and Keith Collins, "How an A.I. 'Cat-and-Mouse Game'

Generates Believable Fake Photos," *New York Times*, Jan. 2, 2018; James Vincent, "New AI Research Makes It Easier to Create Fake Footage of Someone Speaking," *Verge*, July 12, 2017; David Gershgorn, "AI Researchers Are Trying to Combat How AI Can Be Used to Lie and Deceive," *Quartz*, Dec. 8, 2017; *Stanford Encyclopedia of Philosophy*, s.v. "Jean Baudrillard."

8. "THE FIREHOSE OF FALSEHOOD": PROPAGANDA AND FAKE NEWS

135 **"You can sway a thousand men"**: Robert A. Heinlein, "If This Goes On—," in *Revolt in 2100* (New York: Spectrum, 2013), Kindle.

136 **the much lesser known Vladislav Surkov**: Peter Pomerantsev, "Putin's Rasputin," *London Review of Books*, Oct. 20, 2011.

136 **"calculated to evoke hatred"**: V. I. Lenin, "Report to the Fifth Congress of the R.S.D.L.P. on the St. Petersburg Split and the Institution of the Party Tribunal Ensuing Therefrom," in *Lenin Collected Works*, vol. 12 (Moscow: Foreign Languages Publishing House, 1962).

137 **"to an extraordinary degree"**: Anne Applebaum, "100 Years Later, Bolshevism Is Back. And We Should Be Worried," *Washington Post*, Nov. 6, 2017.

138 **"the godfather of what commentators"**: Victor Sebestyen, *Lenin: The Man, the Dictator, and the Master of Terror* (New York: Pantheon Books, 2017), 3.

138 **Steve Bannon, Trump's now estranged**: Ryan Lizza, "Steve Bannon Will Lead Trump's White House," *New Yorker*, Nov. 14, 2016.

138 **The conservative billionaire**: Jane Mayer, "The Reclusive Hedge-Fund Tycoon Behind the Trump Presidency," *New Yorker*, Mar. 27, 2017.

139 **"He offered simple solutions"**: Sebestyen, *Lenin*, 3.

139 **Hitler devoted whole chapters**: "Propaganda: Goebbels' Principles," physics.smu.edu/pseudo/Propaganda/goebbels

.html; Michiko Kakutani, "In 'Hitler,' an Ascent from 'Dunderhead' to Demagogue," *New York Times*, Sept. 27, 2016; Michiko Kakutani, "'How Propaganda Works' Is a Timely Reminder for a Post-Truth Age," *New York Times*, Dec. 26, 2016.

140 **"Who cares whether they laugh"**: Volker Ullrich, *Hitler: Ascent, 1889–1939* (New York: Knopf, 2016), 94. See also Kakutani, "In 'Hitler,' an Ascent from 'Dunderhead' to Demagogue."

140 **"to disrupt the existing order"**: Adolf Hitler, *Mein Kampf* (Boston: Houghton Mifflin, 1943), vol. 2, loc. 10605, Kindle.

140 **"in an ever-changing, incomprehensible world"**: Arendt, *Origins of Totalitarianism*, 382.

141 **"the firehose of falsehood"**: Christopher Paul and Miriam Matthews, "The Russian 'Firehose of Falsehood' Propaganda Model" (Rand Corporation, 2016), 1.

141 **"Russian propaganda makes no commitment"**: Ibid., 5.

142 **Russian propaganda, which was extensively:** Ibid., 3, 4.

143 **"The point of modern propaganda"**: twitter.com /Kasparov63/status/808750564284702720.

143 **"this twittering world"**: T. S. Eliot, *Four Quartets* (New York: Harcourt Brace Jovanovich, 1971), 17.

143 **"In the networked public sphere"**: Zeynep Tufekci, *Twitter and Tear Gas: The Power and Fragility of Networked Protest* (New Haven, Conn.: Yale University Press, 2017), 228–32.

144 **"the real genius"**: Pomerantsev, "Putin's Rasputin."

144 **"He helped invent"**: Peter Pomerantsev, "Russia's Ideology: There Is No Truth," *New York Times*, Dec. 11, 2014.

145 **This same sort of Surkovian manipulation:** Priscilla Alvarez and Taylor Hosking, "The Full Text of Mueller's Indictment of 13 Russians," *Atlantic*, Feb. 16, 2018; Adrian Chen, "The Agency," *New York Times Magazine*, June 2, 2015.

147 **"to keep the great"**: Peter Pomerantsev, "Inside Putin's Information War," *Politico*, Jan. 4, 2015.

147   **"a kitsch Putin-worshipping"**: Pomerantsev, "Putin's Rasputin."

148   **RT published an essay**: Vladislav Surkov, "Crisis of Hypocrisy. 'I Hear America Singing,'" RT, Nov. 7, 2017.

149   **An argument that echoes**: Andrew Sullivan, "The Reactionary Temptation," *New York*, Apr. 30, 2017; Rosie Gray, "Behind the Internet's Anti-Democracy Movement," *Atlantic*, Feb. 10, 2017; Kelefa Sanneh, "Intellectuals for Trump," *New Yorker*, Jan. 9, 2017.

9. THE SCHADENFREUDE OF THE TROLLS

153   **"Attack, attack, attack"**: Marie Brenner, "How Donald Trump and Roy Cohn's Ruthless Symbiosis Changed America," *Vanity Fair*, Aug. 2017.

153   **"The world is a horrible place"**: Donald Trump and Bill Zanker, *Think Big* (New York: HarperCollins, 2009), 174–75.

154   **"My donors are basically saying"**: Rebecca Savransky, "Graham: 'Financial Contributions Will Stop' if GOP Doesn't Pass Tax Reform," *Hill*, Nov. 9, 2017; Cristina Marcos, "GOP Lawmaker: Donors Are Pushing Me to Get Tax Reform Done," *Hill*, Nov. 7, 2017.

154   **"a chaos of peeves"**: Pynchon, *Gravity's Rainbow*, 676.

155   **"They were careless people"**: F. Scott Fitzgerald, *The Great Gatsby* (New York: Oxford University Press, 1998), 142.

156   **The new nihilism is WikiLeaks**: Sue Halpern, "The Nihilism of Julian Assange," *New York Review of Books*, July 13, 2017; Haroon Siddique, "Press Freedom Group Joins Condemnation of WikiLeaks' War Logs," *Guardian*, Aug. 13, 2010; Matthew Weaver, "Afghanistan War Logs: WikiLeaks Urged to Remove Thousands of Names," *Guardian*, Aug. 10, 2010.

156   **upward of ten thousand dollars a month**: Laura Sydell, "We Tracked Down a Fake-News Creator in the Suburbs. Here's

What We Learned," *All Tech Considered*, NPR, Nov. 23, 2016.

157   **"Charge the cockpit":** Publius Decius Mus, "The Flight 93 Election," *Claremont Review of Books*, Sept. 5, 2016; Rosie Gray, "The Populist Nationalist on Trump's National Security Council," *Atlantic*, Mar. 24, 2017; Michael Warren, "The Anonymous Pro-Trump 'Decius' Now Works Inside the White House," *Weekly Standard*, Feb. 2, 2017; Gray, "Behind the Internet's Anti-Democracy Movement."

157   **The new nihilism manifests itself:** Hadley Freeman, "Sandy Hook Father Leonard Pozner on Death Threats: 'I Never Imagined I'd Have to Fight for My Child's Legacy,'" *Guardian*, May 2, 2017; Charles Rabin, "Parkland Students Face New Attack, This Time from the Political Right on Social Media," *Miami Herald*, Feb. 20, 2018.

158   **"Hail Trump! Hail our people!":** Joseph Goldstein, "Alt-Right Gathering Exults in Trump Election with Nazi-Era Salute," *New York Times*, Nov. 20, 2016.

158   **"A 4chan troll":** Marwick and Lewis, *Media Manipulation and Disinformation Online*.

158   **The Huffington Post reported:** Ashley Feinberg, "This Is the Daily Stormer's Playbook," *Huffington Post*, Dec. 13, 2017.

159   **Trump, of course, is a troll:** Amy B Wang, "Trump Retweets Image Depicting 'CNN' Squashed Beneath His Shoe," *Washington Post*, Dec. 24, 2017; twitter.com/realDonaldTrump /status/326970029461614594.

160   **In his revealing 2017 book:** Joshua Green, *Devil's Bargain: Steve Bannon, Donald Trump, and the Storming of the Presidency* (New York: Penguin Press, 2017), 139, 147–48.

161   **"a far too novelistic and bourgeois belief":** Butler, *Postmodernism*, 35.

161   **as David Foster Wallace observed:** "A Conversation with David Foster Wallace by Larry McCaffery," *Review of Contemporary Fiction* 13, no. 2 (Summer 1993); David Foster Wallace, "E Unibus Pluram: Television and U.S. Fiction," *Review of Contemporary Fiction* 13, no. 2 (1993): 151–94.

163   **"You have my word":** Roger Wolmuth, "David Leisure—a.k.a. Joe Isuzu—Finds That the Road to Success Is Paved with Lies, Lies, Lies!," *People,* Nov. 10, 1986.

EPILOGUE

165   **"the technological distractions":** Neil Postman, *Amusing Ourselves to Death* (New York: Penguin, 2006), 156, 141.

165   **"Our priests and presidents":** Ibid., 98.

166   **"Orwell feared those":** Ibid., xix.

166   **too narcotized by "undisguised trivialities":** Ibid., 16.

167   **"aggressive, anxiety-provoking, maudlin":** George Saunders, *The Braindead Megaphone: Essays* (New York: Riverhead Books, 2007), 12, 6, 18.

167   **have made *1984* timely again:** Michiko Kakutani, "Why '1984' Is a 2017 Must-Read," *New York Times,* Jan. 26, 2017.

168   **"further, faster erosion":** Freedom House, "Freedom in the World 2018," freedomhouse.org.

169   **"the 21st-century catastrophe":** Charles McGrath, "No Longer Writing, Philip Roth Still Has Plenty to Say," *New York Times,* Jan. 16, 2018.

169   **"cunning, ambitious, and unprincipled men":** George Washington, "Washington's Farewell Address 1796," avalon.law .yale.edu.

170   **"in common efforts for the common good":** Thomas Jefferson, "First Inaugural Address," Mar. 4, 1801, avalon.law. yale.edu.

171   **serve as "reciprocal checks":** Washington, "Washington's Farewell Address 1796."

172   **"that man may be governed":** Jefferson to John Tyler, June 28, 1804, in *The Papers of Thomas Jefferson,* ed. James P. McClure, vol. 43 (Princeton, N.J.: Princeton University Press, 2017), loc. 18630, Kindle. See also Scott Horton, "Jefferson—Pursuit of the Avenues of Truth," *Browsings* (blog), *Harper's,* Aug. 15, 2009.

172 **"A popular Government"**: James Madison to W. T. Barry, Aug. 4, 1822, in *The Writings of James Madison,* ed. Gaillard Hunt, 9 vols. (New York: G. P. Putnam's Sons, 1900–1910), vol. 9.

ADDITIONAL SOURCES

Arendt, Hannah, *The Human Condition* (Chicago: The University of Chicago Press, 1998).

Avlon, John, *Washington's Farewell: The Founding Father's Warning to Future Generations* (New York: Simon & Schuster, 2017).

Campbell, Jeremy, *The Liar's Tale* (New York: W. W. Norton, 2002).

Chernow, Ron, *Washington: A Life* (New York: Penguin Press, 2010).

Clark, Christopher, *The Sleepwalkers: How Europe Went to War in 1914* (New York: Harper Perennial, 2014).

Confessore, Nicholas, "Cambridge Analytica and Facebook: The Scandal and the Fallout So Far," *New York Times,* Apr. 4, 2018.

D'Antonio, Michael, *The Truth About Trump* (New York: Thomas Dunne Books, 2016).

Diepenbrock, George, "Most Partisans Treat Politics Like Sports Rivalries, Study Shows," *Kansas University Today,* Apr. 15, 2015.

Ellis, Joseph J., *Founding Brothers: The Revolutionary Generation* (New York: Vintage, 2002).

Ellis, Joseph J., *The Quartet: Orchestrating the Second American Revolution, 1783–1789* (New York: Vintage, 2016).

Frum, David, "How to Build an Autocracy," *Atlantic*, March 2017.

Gray, Rosie, "How 2015 Fueled the Rise of the Freewheeling White Nationalist Alt-Movement," *BuzzFeed,* Dec. 27, 2015.

Halpern, Sue, "How He Used Facebook to Win," *New York Review of Books,* June 8, 2017.

Hamilton, Alexander, James Madison, and John Jay, *The Federalist Papers* (Dublin, Ohio: Coventry House Publishing, 2015).

Hofstadter, Richard, *Anti-intellectualism in American Life* (New York: Vintage, 1963).

Hughes, Robert, *Culture of Complaint: The Fraying of America* (New York: Oxford University Press, 1993).

Huxley, Aldous, *Brave New World* (New York: Harper Perennial, 2006).

Ioffe, Julia, "Why Trump's Attack on the Time Warner Merger Is Dangerous for the Press," *Atlantic*, Nov. 28, 2017.

Johnston, David Cay, *The Making of Donald Trump* (Brooklyn: Melville House, 2017).

Kahneman, Daniel, *Thinking, Fast and Slow* (New York: Farrar, Straus and Giroux, 2011).

Kaplan, Fred, *Lincoln: The Biography of a Writer* (New York: Harper, 2008).

Kasparov, Garry, *Winter Is Coming* (New York: PublicAffairs, 2015).

Levi, Primo, *The Drowned and the Saved* (New York: Vintage International, 1989).

Luce, Edward, *The Retreat of Western Liberalism* (New York: Atlantic Monthly Press, 2017).

McCullough, David, *1776* (New York: Simon & Schuster, 2005).

Murphy, Tim, "How Donald Trump Became Conspiracy Theorist in Chief," *Mother Jones*, Nov./Dec. 2016.

O'Brien, Timothy L., *TrumpNation: The Art of Being The Donald* (New York: Grand Central Publishing, 2007).

Pluckrose, Helen, "How French 'Intellectuals' Ruined the West," *Areo*, Mar. 27, 2017.

Pomerantsev, Peter, *Nothing Is True and Everything Is Possible* (New York: PublicAffairs, 2015).

Remnick, David, "A Hundred Days of Trump," *New Yorker*, May 1, 2017.

Ricks, Thomas E., *Fiasco: The American Military Adventure in Iraq* (New York: Penguin Press, 2006).

Rosenberg, Matthew, and Gabriel J.X. Dance, "'You Are the Product': Targeted by Cambridge Analytica on Facebook," *New York Times*, Apr. 8, 2018.

Snyder, Timothy, *On Tyranny* (New York: Tim Duggan Books, 2017).

Stanley, Jason, *How Propaganda Works* (Princeton, N.J.: Princeton University Press, 2015).

Timberg, Carl, Karla Adam and Michael Kranish, "Bannon Oversaw

    Cambridge Analytica's Collection of Facebook Data, According to Former Employee," *Washington Post,* Mar. 20, 2018.

Wolfe, Tom, ed., *The New Journalism* (New York: Picador Books, 1975).

Wolff, Michael, *Fire and Fury: Inside the Trump White House* (New York: Henry Holt & Co., 2018).

Wood, Gordon S., *The Radicalism of the American Revolution* (New York: Vintage, 1993).

Wylie, Christopher, "Why I Broke the Facebook Data Story—and What Should Happen Now," *Guardian,* Apr. 7, 2018.

Yglesias, Matthew, "American Democracy Is Doomed," *Vox,* Oct. 8, 2015.